AIRMAN'S SONG BOOK

For

R. N. H.

AIRMAN'S SONG BOOK

Being an Anthology of Squadron, Concert Party, Training and Camp Songs and Song-Parodies, written by & for Officers, Airmen and Airwomen mainly of the Royal Air Force, its Auxiliaries & its Predecessors, the Royal Flying Corps and the Royal Naval Air Service

Collected, Edited and with an Introduction and Explanatory notes by C. H. WARD-JACKSON, Music edited by LEIGHTON LUCAS And Decorations by BIRO

The whole set out in Chronological Order to present a Historical Picture of the R.A.F. through its Own Songs

William Blackwood & Sons Ltd
Edinburgh & London

1967

Give me the making of the songs of a nation and let who will make its laws.

> —*Epitaph on the gravestone of Henry James Williams who, with Jack Judge, wrote " It's a Long Way to Tipperary."*

S B N 85158 005 x

First printed by the Hollen Street Press, London, W.1 and published by the Sylvan Press Ltd., 24-25 Museum Street, London, W.C.1., in 1945. Second, revised edition printed and reproduced Photo Litho by Latimer Trend & Co. Ltd., Whitstable, Kent, in 1967.

CONTENTS

Songs of the Parachute Regiment

Songs of the Post-War Years 1945-1967

ACKNOWLEDGEMENTS

A book of this kind is essentially the result of the endeavours of many people over many years. My special thanks are due to Group Captain F. D. Tredrey, C.B.E., of William Blackwood & Sons, for initiating this edition and for his comments and advice. My thanks, too, to Lieutenant-General Sir Charles Harington, K.C.B., C.B.E., D.S.O., M.C., for enlisting on my behalf the guidance of the Air Historical Branch of the Ministry of Defence which proved most helpful.

For permission to include the copyright lyrics of several published songs I hasten to acknowledge : the President of the Halton Debating Society (for the Halton apprentices' songs) ; Messrs B. Feldman & Co. (for *We are the A.T.C.*) ; Keith Prowse (for *Bless 'Em All*, published version) ; and the Peter Maurice Music Co. Ltd. (for *If I Only Had Wings* and *My A.C.W.2*.).

For the paratroopers' songs I am indebted to Colonel P. D. F. Thursby, O.B.E., Commandant of the Parachute Regiment Headquarters.

For publishing my requests for songs not included in the earlier edition, I also thank the Editors of *Royal Air Force News*, the Service newspaper, and of *Air Mail*, the Journal of the Royal Air Forces Association.

I would particularly like to acknowledge my debt to the many serving and retired officers, non-commissioned officers, airmen and airwomen, living and dead, who have helped me to form and annotate this collection by bringing to my attention over the past twenty-five years songs of all periods and relevant points of interest. Usually I can be sure only of their names ; their ranks, where I've known them, have been as at the time of my correspondence with them, and their decorations I have known only in one or two cases. They include :—Air Vice-Marshal A.C. Kermode, C.B.E., M.A., F.R.Ae.S. ; Air Commodore Finlay Crerar, C.B.E. ; Group Captains G. M. Knocker and C. L. M. Brown ; Wing Commanders J. Marker, P. A. Gilchrist, P. E. Hadow, R. N. Hesketh, P. H. Holmes, I. J. B. Powell ; Major W. F. Harvey, D.F.C. ; Squadron Leaders E. Dean, G. W. Minto, D. N. Nichols, R. Birley, P. N. L. Nicholson, A. A. Salmon, Charles Bardswell, Victor B. Kendrick, E. A. Vautier, J. A. H. Russell ; Flight Lieutenants W. J. Lonergan, E. W. Thomas, John Mark, J. Maddern Harris, I. F. Anderson, J. A. Atkinson, C. R. Bingham, T. E. Dalton, N. J. Warnes, M.B.E., L.R.A.M., A.R.C.M. ; Flying Officers Arthur Macrae, Paddy Duff, G. A. Turner, Peter Yorke, Wm. Ritchie, C. R. McConnell ; Warrant Officer J. V. C. Claremont ; Sergeants P. Baxter and R. C. Rogers ; and (in absence of knowledge of rank) Messrs. S. A. C. Cawley, John P. Garrad, R. Deal, C. Earnshaw, D. Kelly, John S. Durham, Barker Beresford, Courtney Hume, Gordon Brand and James Beedle.

INTRODUCTION

On April 1, 1968, the Royal Air Force celebrates the fiftieth anniversary of its birthday, so that this is not an inappropriate time to publish this anthology of what might be called some of the minor achievements of that arm of the national defence services, a collection which it has given me pleasure to gather together over the last half of that period.

It was in about 1912, when the Royal Flying Corps was formed, that someone composed and sang the first military flying song, *The Bold Aviator* or *The Dying Airman*, probably at Larkhill on Salisbury Plain. Of its seniority I have been assured by various veterans, and Alan Bott ("Contact") in his flying classic *An Airman's Outings*, published by Blackwood's in 1917, quoted a few lines from it, preceded by—" the somewhat wild evening ends with a sing-song, of which the star number is a ballad to the tune of *The Tarpaulin Jacket* handed down from the pre-war days of the Flying Corps." The song started what became a tradition, and since then airmen have produced a considerable number of distinctive songs, jaunty and boastful at one end of the range, relentlessly ironic at the other. This book is a collection of almost two hundred of them. Arranged chronologically, they constitute a kind of folklore, a history of the spirit of the Royal Air Force and its predecessors.

I started making the collection when my commanding officer asked me if I could find for him various verses of *The Bold Aviator*. I had had a little experience of theatricals, I was making a small study of airmen's colloquialisms and their origins, subsequently published, and soon from various stations to which duty took me I was able to piece together a selection of verses of the song and I could not resist recording others, ancient and modern.

By 1945 these researches into the bacchanalia of flying had resulted in a substantial collection, and it occurred to me that there might be some merit in preparing them for publication. So at the end of the war the collection was published, as it then was, under the present title. Within a short time most of the million people in the Royal Air Force were disbanded, including myself, but I continued to receive lyrics I had overlooked and varied comments from people who had been in the service in war and peace. By then I had become preoccupied with civilian matters, I acknowledged and thanked, filed away and forgot. In time the book went out of print.

Then, twenty years after, came a letter from Frank Tredrey, a director of William Blackwood & Sons. He and the head of the firm, Douglas Blackwood, had both been in the R.A.F. Would I be interested in their publishing a new and revised edition of *The Airman's Songbook* ?

I turned to my old files of correspondence and notes. Their contents had about them the remote scent of all faded papers. There were lyrics and nostalgic reminiscences from almost every rank, but the richest were the oldest—they'd had time to mature. As example I cannot resist quoting one recollection, of the entry into an R.F.C. mess in Flanders of Lieutenant Charles Nungesser, *Escadrille Numéro 65*, a noted pilot of the day :—*Bonjour, messieurs ! Nungesser—moi ! Légion d'Honneur, Croix de Guerre avec soixante palmes, Merito Valore, ze Military Cross ! J'ai abbatu quarante Boches ! Ze ozzer day I come in and I make ze bad landing. I say " Pouf ! it is only ze chassis !"   And zen I look and it is ze whole bloody lot ! But nevair mind !   Today I take off ze wheel—tomorrow 'oo knows ? Nungesser—c'est moi !*   And, perhaps more to the point, another memory, of a lyric-writing pilot, Lieutenant J. C. Whittaker, who " arranged a board and notebook to strap on his knee, and wrote most of them over the lines on patrol."

I had in my files the material for many additions to the collection, but *all* were pre-1945. What songs, if any, had been originated since that time ? I renewed old acquaintanceships and friendships, sought new ones, obtained official help and advice, wrote an appeal to the editors of the *Royal Air Force News* and *Air Mail*. But the answer almost invariably was : " It's always the old songs we sing." In time I added a few post-war songs and the collection assumed its present extent and form, with the invaluable aid of my music collaborator Leighton Lucas, the composer, conductor and one-time R.A.F. music instructor. Readers may recall his superb incidental music for what is perhaps the finest war-time flying film, *Target for Tonight*.

What is an airman's song ? I would define it as a lyric *by, for* and *about* airmen or their activities. It must be homemade. I exclude scripts written professionally though not necessarily those by professionals. I exclude the bawdy stag party song. It is not peculiar to airmen. The words must be *by, for* and *about* airmen, but the tune may come from anywhere.

It is natural that, with a few exceptions, airmen's songs are not sung to original music but plunder or parody hymns, folk songs and airs popular at the time. The reasons are clear : there are so many excellent tunes to select from that it is not difficult to find one that fits the desired mood ; rhymesters are commoner than music composers ; it is easier to record and memorise original lines than an original tune (if such a thing as that exists) ; and so many songs are written as an outcome of and under conditions where the only instrument available is primitive. Very often too a hymn tune or the air of a popular song will almost *demand* that new lines be written for it that are more appropriate to the occasion.

In their songs airmen have written their own history, and the scenes of their attempts at composition are scattered across the world : around an iron stove in a nissen hut in Iceland, in a bivouac on a Sudan landing ground, in a canteen in Kent on a " commando " piano, on the banks of the Tigris, in a flying training mess in Saskatchewan, in an apprentices' school in beechy Buckinghamshire, in a stony waste on the North-west Frontier of India, squatting on a petrol tin in the Libyan sand, at the Cadet College at Cranwell, in the hot-flannel heat of West Africa, back of barbed wire in a German *stalag*, in the arid Arakan, in an *estaminet* in Flanders.

The best songs have come from times and places denied other forms of fun, remote and distant places far away from home, wives and families. The improvised field conditions in Flanders in the early years of the first World War certainly gave this kind of thing a boost in the R.F.C. days ; the songs of that time have a quality never excelled. And, in 1960, at the other end of the half-century, it was not by chance that *The Song of the Two Sad Flight Sergeants*—the *Gan Song*—came out of a station in the Indian Ocean 2,500 miles away from Singapore and a similar distance from Aden a march song original both in lyric and tune.

Many of these songs were not so much composed as evolved over a long period and often in various places. Most people would say (for example) that *Bless 'Em All* dates from the second World War and they probably would not particularly connect it with flying. Yet it has been the unofficial trooping song of the R.A.F. from its beginning in 1918. During the broadcast of the R.A.F.'s 25th birthday anniversary celebrations in 1943 Mr S. P. B. Mais (ex-R.F.C.) pointed out that it in fact originated in the Royal Naval Air Service, written in 1916 by Fred Godfrey. That version was not for publication, and it was unknown to the public till the late 1930's when it appeared in a completely clean pinafore. Meanwhile, airmen had put all kinds of words to it, the essence of which is not unfairly reflected in the published version.

Another example of song evolution is the ditty first put to the tune of the old ballad *The Mountains of Mourne* in the Air Battalion of the Royal Engineers in 1911, amended in 1912 with the absorption of that body of men into the new R.F.C., then evolving to a later form in 1916.

Another case history is of *Western Desert Madness*, typical of the kind of song that grows out of operational conditions.

Here is a description, as I received it, of how it was written :
" It was thought of by a flight lieutenant D.F.C. who, with
two sergeant pilots (D.F.M. and dead), wrote the first verse
at Antelat in December, 1941. The first verse is confined to
the advance from Fort Maddalena on the wire up to Msus,
when we lived entirely on bully beef, biscuits and marmalade.
We were equipped with very tired Hurricane Ones and had
many a good dogfight with the 109's. We were always being
promised Hurricane Two's or better, but never got 'em.

" The ' crouching in the wadi ' was due to the normal call
of nature in the morning, not to sniping. It was a ' brave '
sight to see the squadron getting down to it. Our tea
invariably tasted of petrol or salt depending on where we
stopped—salt at Tobruk and Gazala, petrol at Msus.

" The second and third verses were written at Martuba
by all of us. We played them on a piano we found at
Benghazi, which went everywhere with us, both on retreats
and advances. As you can see, it is pretty bitter towards the
soldiers, but you may recall there was a hectic retreat in
January 1942. We were left behind at Benghazi to cover the
4th Indian Division, and very nearly spent the rest of the war
in a prison camp.

" But back to the song. ' That man again ' was an extra-
ordinarily pleasant major from a Highland regiment who used
to turn up at dawn and ask us to go ground strafing the
advancing Hun. The third and fourth lines are self-evident,
as we were given a ' backs to the wall ' order. We had one
magnificent day of ground strafing when we hacked up a
large column of Huns and enabled the 4th Indian Division
to withdraw—hence the reference to Benina, our aerodrome.

" The last verse, in line three, has a crack at ' Mary '
Coningham, when he was worried that we weren't getting
newspapers—and all we wanted was aircraft, petrol and
ammo. The ' promise of Tomahawks ' given ' on loan '
refers to our stay at Benghazi, when we were being
re-equipped with No. 4 South African Air Force Squadron's
' Tommies ' and they were getting our ' Hurries.' The
moment the flap started we had to return to our ' Hurries '
in which we fought our way back via Martuba to Gazala."

It may be said that there are four classifications of airman's
song : Squadron, Concert Party, Training and Camp Songs.
The first and pre-eminent are born out of squadron get-
togethers of one kind or another, written in the main on
operations, and typical are *I Left the Mess Room Early*
(R.N.A.S. 1914-18), *The Ballad of Sulaiman* (the ' Peace '
Years), and *The Firth of Flaming Forth* (Coastal Command,
second World War).

A squadron song does not need to be " of " a particular squadron. Few have retained identity exclusively with any single unit. It is rarely possible to say for sure whether any particular song *belongs* to anyone. Usually the words are composed communally, everyone taking a hand ; or the author and his collaborators have not survived and no record has been kept. Different squadrons sing different versions of the same song, they get carried from one mess to another through visits and postings ; and only exceptionally do they achieve definitive form. So if in this anthology I have mentioned certain squadrons in relation to particular songs it does not mean necessarily that they originated them. Also, while I have inserted the names of some authors (and their claims may be tenuous), in most cases they have been aided by others.

The Concert Party group describes itself—songs written by airmen, about airmen to sing to airmen on the station stage in home-made theatricals. Where squadron ditties draw their airs chiefly from traditional or music-hall songs, or from hymns, the composer of the concert party song tends to borrow from musical shows of the time or even to rise to the luxury of an original tune. Examples are : *There's no A.M.O. about Love ; My Motter ; The Stately Dromes of England ;* and the *Song of the Two Sad Flight Sergeants.* These lyrics are among the cleverest and wittiest, though their very sophistication renders them less suitable for singing *tout ensemble* than for the skilled soloist, and they consequently are known to fewer people than the communally-written ruthless rhymes. However, the original march tune of *The Gan Song* surely deserves to be played by R.A.F. bands everywhere.

The third category is Training Songs—those of the aircraft-apprentices' school at Halton are outstanding, and other examples are *The Cadet* (a pretty Cranwell picture of the 1920's), *Heaven or Hell*, and *The Song of the A.T.C.*

Under Camp Songs I classify those that bear the mark of origin in canteen, Naafi and barrack hut, songs that belong essentially to the aircraftman, the airc or erk. In this class fall the *Service Police Song, Song of the Shirt, Africa Star*—and *Bless 'Em All.*

I have also included a few things which stand alone and cannot be classified at all. A notable example, in serious vein, is the *Hymn to Airmen* written by Air Vice-Marshal E. B. C. Betts in London 1940 and subsequently sung at Battle of Britain and other services. I trust that the chaplains will pardon me for including, at the other end of the scale, that masterly piece of irreverence *A Service of Thanksgiving for Safe Arrival in Iraq.* I have also included that totally different kind of exercise in irony, *The " Peace " of Waziristan.* They are all essential parts of this folk-lore.

Why are airmen's songs written and sung ? On the face of it, to entertain parties and audiences often far removed from all but home-made amusement ; but, fundamentally, to " let off steam." ˙ Often they are produced by a kind of emotional spontaneous combustion, especially the squadron and camp songs. Without design someone idly plays or whistles a hymn tune. Someone else adds a few words— *From Greenland's icy mountains, from India's coral strand.* Perhaps another recalls a word or two from the other hymn to this air, *The Church's One Foundation.* But, rejecting all these words because they simply do not express the truth of the moment, the music almost *compels* the production of substitutes, and someone pipes up—*The nissen hut's foundation is petrol tins galore.* Someone else adds—*They are the one salvation of troops on Iceland's shore.* That leads naturally to—*One tin to shave your face in, one tin to brew your tea.* And the party then explodes into—*One tin is your wash basin, One tin your lavatory* or something like it. Signals and intelligence officers often bring to play a verbal skill that others in the party lack, and soon there is born a parody, though it may more aptly be described as a folk-song-in-the-making since there is rarely any conscious attempt to burlesque the original ; the original is used merely as a skeleton on which to build something quite different. The wittiest songs of the concert party type are not produced in this communal way, the niceties of their composition demand detachment, whereas most songs that are closest to the spirit of the moment are so produced.

Occasionally airmen's songs are jingoist asseverations that make all but the tipsy blush (*We'll defend your blue skies, over land and sea*). Rarely they take the form of a lament (*So when again 'neath peaceful skies the Royal Air Force daily flies, Think of the boy whose body lies at Kairouan, at Kairouan*). Often they are narratives (*They sent us out to Egypt, a green and pleasant land*). They long for peace and home (*Roll on the Boat.*) And of some aircraft they can be even affectionate (*There's an old-fashioned Bristol with old-fashioned planes*). But, overwhelmingly, they deal with death and dismemberment of man and machine, the theme of the most typical, the key for which was set fifty years ago by *The Bold Aviator.* They divide in deep distrust between unreliable equipment and remote authority. They are essentially the by-product of fear and frustration—of sudden death, maiming, separation from family and friends, boredom, " hot air "—and of the need to get them out of your system by laughter, ridicule, grousing, cursing, bawling, blasphemy and by any other way you can ; like a baby, give vent. When airmen's songs grumble they are far more successful than when they sing of agreeable things. They rarely deride the enemy, more often reflect fear of him. And of romance, sentiment ?— there's scarcely a murmur. There is no equivalent of that wistful little lady underneath the lamplight, Lili Marlene.

Some reviewers of the earlier edition of this anthology noted that the words of airmen's songs are less naive, and their parodies wittier, than those of the older services. Certainly the intricate mechanisms of aircraft and the virtues and faults of various types yield subjects for ingenious rhyming. That makes them more amusing to read, if less suitable for community singing. Another characteristic rendering them more obscure to the layman is that they are peppered with colloquialisms peculiar to flying. As early as 1930 the apprentices at Halton were singing :

> *It has been true, I'm told, ever since the days of old,*
> *That the language which we use is apt to vary,*
> *And the slang which we invent*
> *Will form a supplement*
> *To the next issue of the Oxford Dictionary.*

Wherever I have felt it necessary I have given footnote definitions, but I would refer the uninitiated though interested to the glossary of slang and specialist terms at the end of the book, as this may assist them to comprehend the apparently incomprehensible.

It goes almost without saying that the original versions of a large number of airmen's songs are as full of swear-words as there are sultanas in a piece of Dundee cake. Especially is this so of squadron and camp songs. It is equally obvious that the expletives are relished by the singing airman as much as the schoolboy delights in the sultanas. No doubt many veterans will cry tears when they glance over the versions here printed and taste the cack-handed cooking which many of them have undergone to fit them for publication. Yet I felt it best to slip in euphemisms in many cases, knowing full well that they would be ignored, in appropriate company, and the originals replaced in all their fruity glory.

It is true that, where twenty years ago four-letter words were in the main unprintable, public taste today permits them in certain contexts. In this edition I could have reverted to the " originals " of some songs, first airborne in various shades of blue, from cerulean to indigo. I have not done so for two reasons. First, it would have been out of keeping with the traditions of my publisher (which reach back to the Napoleonic wars, and are Scots withal). Second, the words of these songs were put together for singing, not for speaking, let alone reading ; and the four-letter word, when read, attracts far more attention than when spoken ; and when spoken carries more weight, regardless of vocal volume, than when sung—anyway under party conditions. The permanence of type lends the printed swear-word an artificial and exaggerated authority. So, though to euphemise is to distort, I believe there is rather less distortion in the euphemisms I have used than there would have been had I *printed*, for all and sundry, words that were originally *sung* in a special context of circumstances.

However, it has gone against the grain to have had to expunge words that are in such common aviation-use that, within that circle, they are not improper yet, outside it, are more than impolite. I refer to such expressions as the standard English used by airmen for mist, fog, bad weather, *flak* or any such phenomena that hinders the orderly progress of an aircraft through space.

My apologies, then, to anyone who feels that I may have Gone Too Far (there cannot be many) and to others who feel that I have Not Gone Far Enough. So don't shoot the pianist, he's done his best. At the same time I like the story of one correspondent who wrote : " I spent a night at T——— recently when a party was on for a visiting squadron, and most of the old songs were sung with extraordinary solemnity by young men holding their cans of beer like oblations or ritual sacrifices, and the songs seemed obscener than ever— almost sublimely so. I remember years ago discussing Rabelais with Dr J. A. Richards, the literary critic, and some rather prim undergraduate said, ' After reading Rabelais I feel I want to have a bath '. ' Really,' said Richards, 'do you know, I always feel I've had one.' " At the same time I need hardly apologise to any disappointed reader who expected to find in this anthology such masterpieces of bawdry as *Salome* in the original, *Lulu, The Ballad of Eskimo Nell, Mussolini's Organ Grinders*, and *There's a Street in Cairo Full of Grief and Shame*. They do not come within my definition of airmen's songs, however many nissens they may have shaken.

Written collections of airmen's songs are rare and scattered. The circumstances in which most songs have been produced and sung are not conducive to order. Nevertheless, a few squadrons had in years gone by, and may still have, their often self-appointed Custodian of the Squadron Song-book, and to a number of these I am indebted for " collector's pieces," for dates and other information. There are also a number of collections in the U.S.A. of songs of the U.S. Air Corps. And, perhaps because I did not try hard enough, I never succeeded in obtaining a *Luftwaffe* song-book officially issued during the war to German airmen. But these, anyway, fall outside my scope.

Few collections have ever reached the permanence of print, but there are some. First, a collection of twenty-six R.F.C. and R.N.A.S. songs was included in *Tommy's Tunes*, edited and arranged by Lieutenant F. T. Nettleingham, R.F.C., and published in 1917 by Erskine MacDonald, Ltd. These included songs that had been printed in *Aeronautics* during the first World War, and also in *Flying*. Incidentally, Nettleingham referred to the R.F.C. as " the writer's corps " and there is no doubt that the novelty of flying attracted an unusually high proportion of writers to it in those early days. This may account for the literary skill apparent in many of the first war lyrics.

Then in those days 54 Squadron was widely known for its songs. Lieutenant-Colonel L. A. Strange, in his *Recollections of an Airman*, recalls that it was commanded by Major Maxwell and came under 80th Wing. " The spirit of this squadron," said Strange, " is happily caught by the songs they produced and sang in the mess ; some of these have been printed in a little book." That little book, long since a rarity, was called *Cinquante Quatre*, at first privately printed in 1917 and later published by Bowes & Bowes, Cambridge. It contained ten songs of the squadron.

Another record is *Air Force Songs and Verses*, published by Aeronautics Ltd., in 1927, containing, in addition to the 54 Squadron songs, twenty-seven others of the 1914-18 period. A collection was also brought together years ago for 22 Squadron, a history of which has been written by Major W. F. J. Harvey ; and another for 43 Squadron, James Beedle's history of which was recently published.

In one version or another most of the songs in the foregoing records will be found in the present anthology.

A further record : *The Halton Song Book*, songs sung by the aircraft-apprentices during the inter-war years, " the Long Weekend " as Charles Graves called them. The book was printed for the Halton Debating Society in 1930, it contains thirty-two original songs written for station theatricals, and forms in itself an excellent picture of life at the apprentices' school founded there from a mechanics' wing in 1925. Another printed collection came out of Halton in 1935, *Songs for Halton & the Royal Air Force*, containing the original songs and others.

Many of these Halton apprentices' songs were written by Air Vice-Marshal A. C. Kermode, who became Director of Educational Services at the Air Ministry. He had much to do with the song tradition from the time he was in the R.N.A.S. in the first World War. He was the prime mover behind a series of comic operas at Halton, an idea that was developed in the war on a larger, professional scale by Ralph Reader, and his "Gang Shows"—entertainers-in-uniform, toured from the Air Ministry to stations at home and overseas. They most successfully grafted on to the R.A.F. the techniques of Reader's earlier " Gang Shows " for the Boy Scout Movement. Where E.N.S.A. provided professional entertainment from the outside, the Gang Shows provided it from within.

The R.A.F. song tradition infiltrated our first parachute troops, jointly trained and organised by R.A.F. and Army. For example, as they took off for the first operation of its kind, February, 1941, Southern Italy, the parachutists sang a song specially composed for the occasion. Today surviving copies of *Parachutist Song Hits*, a booklet printed for the Parachute Regimental Association, are rare, and I am indebted to Colonel P. D. F. Thursby, O.B.E., for permission to quote from it at the close of the second World War section. The songs have much the same quality as the air-force songs, and some are obvious variants.

The only other printed records I know (apart from one or two published in sheet music form) are in the autobiographies and diaries of pilots and others, and scattered through the pages of station and squadron magazines and flying publications.

It is natural that peace-time produces fewer songs than war-time. Fewer men are engaged, conditions of service are less rigorous ; also the professional airman, commissioned or otherwise, is anyway more used to service conditions than the civilian-in-uniform, and is in less need of the kind of relief that singing and song-making give. Of course, this is a generalisation, and in peace, exceptionally, squadrons are on active service under conditions often tougher than many are in war. But the numbers involved are very small.

It is also not surprising that the last twenty years have been a good deal less productive of songs than the inter-war years. The leisure hours of society generally have undergone great change. People no longer make their own amusements. The cinematograph, dating from the same time as the aeroplane, ushered in a period of mass-produced, mass-communicated entertainment. Broadcasting pushed the movement further. Now television is the most insatiable leisure-consumer of all. Where, in the days of those magnificent men in their flying machines, they gravitated to the mess piano of an evening, today they do much the same as most other people at a loose end—they watch the images and listen to the voices of others.

Moreover, since the de-rationing of petrol in 1950 mess life, out of which these songs are born, has become less influential than it was. The proportion of married men in the service must be much higher today than between the wars. Fewer are separated from wives and families. More bachelors are posted near home. And of course better pay and allowances relative to civilian have reduced the extent to which all ranks are thrown onto their own resources when not on duty.

Overseas also there are considerable social differences. The married man posted abroad with wife and family is now a commonplace, and because of the speed and frequency of air transport and the rapidity of mails few men serving their overseas tour are as remote as many were before 1939.

In short, most of the frustrations that gave rise to the songs that let off steam now scarcely exist. The steam is no longer there.

Yet the old songs are still sung, at mess parties, at reunions of one kind and another, and wherever airmen and ex-airmen foregather. Also I hope there will be sufficient interest in this anthology to justify its publication on rather firmer grounds than those of fun and games. To those serving in the Royal Air Force the songs should be a source of inspiration and understanding, a record of their folk-lore, an illuminant of the most vital element of any fighting force, morale. To those who have retired from service the songs should, rather like an album of old snapshots, re-awaken memories and provoke reflection. Certainly it is a book that can be easily dipped into, yet I hope that above all it will be read as an account, written in their own words, of the spirit of the men and women who, over fifty years, have worn the uniforms and flown the aircraft of our youngest armed service.

C. H. WARD-JACKSON

Polruan, Cornwall
February 1967

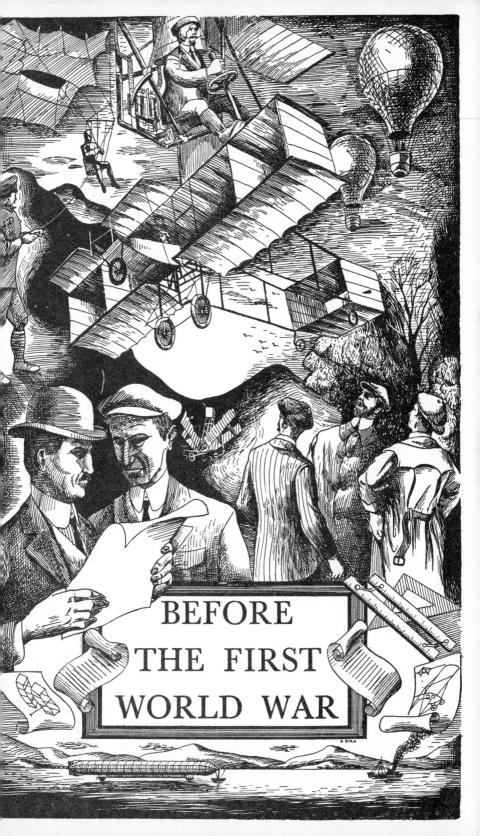

BEFORE
THE FIRST
WORLD WAR

This is the oldest squadron song of all, and the best known. It certainly goes back to the beginning of the Royal Flying Corps in 1912, and possibly to the formation in 1911 of the Air Battalion of the Royal Engineers from the R.E.'s Balloon Company. It was sung by most squadron messes in 1914-18. The original verse and chorus are marked with asterisks; the others have been added by various squadrons chiefly in the 1914-18 period. Sung to the tune of "The Tarpaulin Jacket."

THE BOLD AVIATOR
or
THE DYING AIRMAN

*Oh, the bold aviator was dying,
And as 'neath the wreck-age he lay, he lay,
To the sobbing me-chanics about him
These last parting words he did say:

Chorus:
      Two valve springs you'll find in my stomach,
      Three spark plugs are safe in my lung (my lung),
      The prop is in splinters inside me,
      To my fingers the joy-stick has clung.

Oh, had I the wings of a little dove,
Far a-way, far a-way would I fly, I fly,
Straight to the arms of my true love,
And there would I lay me and die.
      Take the propeller boss out of my liver,
      Take the aileron out of my thigh (my thigh)
      From the seat of my pants take the piston,
      Then see if the old crate will fly.

Then get you two little white tombstones,
Put them one at my head and my toe, my toe,
And get you a pen-knife and scratch there,
" Here lies a poor pilot below".
      *Take the cylinders out of my kidneys,
      The connecting rod out of my brain (my brain),
      From the small of my back get the crankshaft,
      And assemble the en-gyne again.

And get you six brandies and sodas,
And lay them all out in a row,
And get you six other good airmen,
To drink to this pilot below. Oh—
      Take the cylinders out of my kidneys
      The connecting rod out of my brain (my brain),
      From the small of my back take the crankshaft,
      And assemble the en-gyne again.

And when at the Court of Enquiry
They ask for the reason I died, I died,
Please say I forgot twice iota
Was the minimum angle of glide. Oh—
      Take the cylinders out of my kidneys
      The connecting rod out of my brain (my brain),
      From the small of my back take the crankshaft,
      And assemble the en-gyne again.

And when I join the Air Force
Way, way up in the sky, the sky,
Let's hope that they know twice iota
Is the minimum angle to fly. Oh—
>Take the cylinders out of my kidneys
>The connecting rod out of my brain (my brain),
>From the small of my back take the crankshaft,
>And assemble the en-gyne again.

Another version:

A poor aviator lay dying
At the end of a bright summer's day,
His comrades were gathered around him
To carry the fragments away.

>*Chorus*:
>The engine was piled on his wishbone,
>The Hotchkiss was wrapped round his head,
>A spark plug stuck out of each elbow,
>It was plain that he'd shortly be dead.

He spat out a valve and a gasket,
And stirred in the sump where he lay,
And turning, then, to his companions,
These last parting words he did say :
>Take the manifold out of my larynx,
>The butterfly valve from my neck,
>Remove from my kidneys the camrods,
>There's a lot of good parts in the wreck.

Take the piston rings out of my stomach,
And the cylinders out of my brain,
Extract from my liver the crankshaft,
And assemble the engine again.
>I'll be riding a-cloud in the morning,
>With no rotary for me to cuss,
>Shake the lead from your feet and get busy,
>There's another lad wanting this bus.

Who minds to the dust returning?
Who shrinks from the sable shore
Where the high and lofty yearning
Of the soul shall be no more?
>So stand to your glasses steady,
>This world is a world full of lies,
>Here's a health to the dead already,
>And Hurrah for the next man who dies.

4

Another version :

The Young Aviator lay dying,
   And as in the hangar he lay, he lay,
To the mechanics who round him were standing
   These last parting words he did say :

Chorus: Take the cylinders out of my kidneys,
         The connecting rod out of my brain, my brain,
      From the small of my back take the camshaft,
         And assemble the engine again.

Then go ye and get me a school-bus,
   And bury me out on the Plain, the Plain,
And get them to write on my tombstone
   Some Formulæ out of Duchesne.

When the Court of Enquiry assembles
   To find out the reason I died, I died,
Then say I forgot " Twice Iota "
   Was the minimum angle of glide.

Oh, had I the wings of an Avro
   Then far into Holland I'd fly, I'd fly,
I'd stop there until the war's over
   And laugh at you blighters on high.

And now I suppose I'll be joining
   The Flying Corps up in the sky, the sky,
Where they all understand " Twice Iota "
   And they all have got wings that will fly.

5

R·F·C· R·N·A·S·

FROM 1914 TO THE
ARMISTICE IN 1918

Dating from 1915-16, *an air mechanic's song.* " *Thirty chest* " *means thirty-inch measurement* ; *two-bob a day was the pay of a second-class air mechanic* ; *four-bob was that of a first-class mechanic, and* " *first* " *refers to promotion from second to first class.* *Larkhill was at one time a training ground for drill, etc.*

A RECRUITING SONG OF THE
ROYAL FLYING CORPS

I was standing at the corner
    When I heard somebody say,
" Come and join the Flying Corps—
    Come, step along this way."
I threw my thirty-chest out,
    And put my cap on straight,
And walked into the office
    Along with Jack, my mate.

They offered me two bob a day,
    I said, " I didn't think,"
But when they murmured " Four bob,"
    I said, " Come, have a drink."
And now I spend my Sundays
    With Lizzie in the Lane.
I wonder when I'll get my first
    Or see an aeroplane.

I never was so well off
    In all my naturel :
You should see me in St. James's,
    I am an awful swell.
And now I've been to Larkhill
    My education is complete.
" Form fours," " 'Bout turn," " Two deep,"
    Oh ! don't I do it neat !

You should see us hold our heads up
    When the others pass us by.
The girls they all run after us
    And, breathless, say, " Oh, my !
Dear Tommy brave, I'll be your slave,
    If you will take me up."
But hastily I answer,
    " I've an invitation out to sup."

Sung with gusto by R.F.C. officers and men alike—typical of the days when the air force wore the "maternity jacket" and the "split-arse" cap. 1915.

THE RAGTIME FLYING CORPS

go out   all the people roar,   We are the Ragtime Fly-ing Corps.

We are the Ragtime Flying Corps,
We are the ragtime boys,
We are respected by every nation,
And we're loved by all the girls (I don't think).
People, they think we're millionaires,
Think we're dealers in stocks and shares ;
When we go out all the people roar,
We are the Ragtime Flying Corps.

We are the Ragtime Flying Corps,
We are the R.F.C.
We spend our tanners, we know our manners,
And are respected wherever we go.
Walking up and down the Farnborough Road,
Doors and windows open wide.
We are the boys of the R.F.C.
We don't care a damn for Germany ;
We are the Flying Corps.

This parody exemplifies song evolution. In 1910, when the published ballad was almost unknown, it was parodied by I. J. B. Powell (later Wing Commander) when he joined the Royal Engineers, then recruiting pioneers :—

THE MOUNTAINS OF MOURNE

Now don't be alarmed at the next news, my dear,
I've joined the R.E., a full-blown pioneer.
They said when I 'listed, " A Sergeant you'll be,"
But divil a bit of the Sergeant I see.
And these Drill Instructors they bawl and they shout,
But I can't tell a word what they're talking about,
And if things don't alter I'll ruddy soon be
Where the Mountains of Mourne sweep down to the Sea.

Early in 1914 when Powell transferred, along with others from the Royal Engineers, to the new Royal Flying Corps, he adapted the verse to fit the times :—

Now ere I have finished, just one item more,
I'm a 2nd A.M. in the Royal Flying Corps.
They said, when I 'listed, " A Pilot you'll be "
But divil a bit of the pilot I see.
And these Sergeant Majors they bawl and they shout,
But I can't tell a word what they're talking about.
And if things don't alter I'll ruddy soon be
Where the Mountains of Mourne sweep down to the Sea.

By 1916 the lines had evolved to the following definitive form :—
Dear mother, I'm writing this letter, you see ;
I'm second A.M. in the R.F.C.
And when I enlisted, a pilot to be ;
But oh ! 'tis never a bit of the flying I see.
The Sergeant Majors they bawl and they shout,
They don't never know what they're talking about.
Now if things don't alter I'll blooming soon be
Where the Mountains of Mourne sweep down to the Sea.

Dating from early 1916, 25 *Squadron, R.F.C., and written by Lieutenant J. C. Whittaker, pilot, for a camp revue " Hun Likely."*

THE AIR-CREW'S WISH

When hill and dale with snow are clad,
  And frost is in the air,
The " dud " days come to make us glad,
  " Hot air gaps " everywhere.

And so, what can I do but say,
  " I hope the clouds will cling
A hundred feet or lower each day
  All through the coming spring."

Aside : By the Air Mechanics :
Those who bend 'em
Don't have to mend 'em.

———

Another R.F.C. recruiting song, about 1916. *Pope and Bradley, the tailors, were early specialists in making the R.F.C. tunic or " maternity jacket." To the tune of " The Lowther Arcade and the Tin Gee-gee,"*

ANOTHER RECRUITING SONG OF THE ROYAL FLYING CORPS

I was walking in Town up Regent Street
  When I saw the R.F.C.
I thought to myself—Now, they look neat,
  I think that would suit me.
So I strolled inside, and carefully lied
  About my carpentry,
But when I came out, I swaggered about—
  For I was in the R.F.C.

They sent me down to Salisbury Plain
  To a place they call Larkhill.
The sergeants they bullied with might and main
  And made us do some drill.
All the fellows they were " risky," they smoked but De Reszke
  When going to the Y.H. hut.
And they didn't do us badly—tho' we weren't from Pope and
    Bradley—
  For we're the Flying Corps—Tut ! Tut !

Another R.F.C. mess song-parody. Rumpety = Maurice Farman Shorthorn aircraft. Sung to the tune of "What Do You Want To Fool Around Like That For?"

WHAT DO YOU WANT . . . . ?

What do you want to go and crash like that for?
It's the second time today.
You make me sad—you make me mad,
First it was a Rumpety, then a brand new Spad.

What do you want to fool around like that for?
First you banked, and then you slipped away.

But never mind, you'll go up again tonight
With umpteen bombs, all loaded with dynamite.
Then if you make another crash like last time,
Well, you won't draw next week's pay.

———

The R.F.C. version of a song sung throughout the Services in the First World War and still occasionally heard. There is a peace-time flying training version, see page 98.

WHEN THIS RUDDY WAR IS OVER

When this ruddy war is over,
   O! how happy I shall be!
When this ruddy war is over
   And we come back from Germany.
No more blooming kit inspection,
   No more church parade for me.
When this ruddy war is over
   You can have your R.F.C.

When this ruddy war is over
   O! how happy we shall be!
When this ruddy war is over
   And we come back from Germany.
Roll on, when we go on furlough ;
   Roll on, when we go on leave,
Then we'll catch the train for Blighty,
   Though we'll leave the girls bereaved.

A Great War parody (about 1916) *of the* 23rd *Psalm of David. The reference to* " R.A.F." *means, not* " Royal Air Force" *but* " Royal Aircraft Factory engine."*

THE PILOT'S PSALM

The B.E.2C is my bus ; therefore shall I want.
He maketh me to come down in green pastures.
He leadeth me where I will not go.
He maketh me to be sick ; he leadeth me astray on all cross country
    flights.
Yea, though I fly o'er No-man's Land where mine enemies would
    compass me about, I fear much evil for *thou* art with me ; thy
    joystick and thy prop discomfort me.
Thou preparest a crash before me in the presence of mine enemies ;
    thy R.A.F. anointeth my hair with oil, thy tank leaketh badly.
Surely to goodness thou shalt not follow me all the days of my life ;
    else I shall dwell in the House of Colney Hatch for ever.

Sung with mock seriousness by most R.F.C. squadrons from 1916.

WHO KILLED COCK ROBIN ?

Who killed Cock Robin?
  " I," said the Hun,
  " With my Lewis gun,
I killed Cock Robin."

All the planes in the air
Went a-dipping and a-throbbing,
When they heard of the death of poor Cock Robin,
When they heard of the death of poor Cock Robin.

Who saw him hit?
  " I," said old Fritz,
  " And I have a bit,
I saw him hit."

And all the planes in the air
Went a-swaying and a-bobbing,
When they heard of the death of poor Cock Robin,
When they heard of the death of poor Cock Robin.

Who saw him die?
  " I," said the spy,
  " With my telepathic eye,
I saw him die."

And all the planes in the air
Went a-straffing and a-bombing,
When they heard of the death of poor Cock Robin,
When they heard of the death of poor Cock Robin.

Sung in 1916 by 3 Squadron at Narborough, Norfolk, to the tune of "Good-bye-ee, Don't Cry-ee."

THREE SQUADRON

We're Three-ee, Yes Three-ee,
And we're right at the top of the Tree-ee.
Where the green leaves always grow.
We're just tickled to death to go.
We fly-ee, so high-ee,
We're the only master of the sky-ee.
Bon Soir, old thing,
Cheerio, One Wing !
Napoo, Not Two, We're Three-ee.

A parody of a popular music-hall song of the day sung by Twenty-second Squadron and others around 1916. To the ragtime tune "He's a Cousin of Mine."

WE HAVEN'T SEEN THE SERGEANT

We haven't seen the sergeant for a hell of a time,
We haven't seen the sergeant for a hell of a time.
We came to Farnborough to see what he was doing,
Twenty-second Squadron will be his ruddy ruin.
We haven't seen the sergeant for a hell of a time—
Perhaps he's been blown up by a mine
(Let's hope so).
He's the leader of the cookhouse gang
So, curse him, he's no cousin of mine.

An observers' song to the tune of " Think of Me" from the musical comedy " Yes, Uncle."

BACK SEAT BALLAD

Think of me when your pressure's falling,
And you're almost stalling off the ground.
    Think of me when your engine's stuttering,
    And my heart is fluttering at the beastly sound.
Think of me when you crash on landing,
And your " understanding " comes away,
Say you always think of me
For I'm thinking of you all day.

———

An R.F.C. parody of a famous Great War song. B.E.2Cs were an aircraft of Government design, not over-popular, and the " Raf" was their engine produced by the Royal Aircraft Factory. To the tune of " Keep the Home Fires Burning."

NAPOO-FINI !

Keep the 2Cs turning.
Watch the windsticks squirming,
The Raf has chugged his inside out,
All on his blooming own.
Can't yer 'ear it grinding?
'Oo the 'ell's a-pining?
Don't yer 'ear the fabric rip?—
List ter its sad, sad moan !

This parody was sung in almost every R.F.C. mess. Fred Karno was the leading music-hall impresario of the day, of the ragtime or " crazy gang " variety, first mentor of Charlie Chaplin. Sung to the tune of " The Church's One Foundation."

FRED KARNO'S AIR CORPS

We are Fred Kar - no's Air Corps; we are the R. F. C. We can - not fly, we can - not shoot, what rud - dy use are we? But when we get to Ber - lin, the Kai - ser he will say, Hoch! Hoch! Mein Gott! What a rud-dy fine lot are the boys of the R. F. C.

We are Fred Karno's air corps,
We are the R.F.C.
We cannot fly,
We cannot shoot,
What ruddy use are we?
But when we get to Berlin
The Kaiser he will say,
" Hoch ! Hoch ! Mein Gott !
What a ruddy fine lot
Are the boys of the R.F.C.."

Opening chorus of a camp revue, early 1916, *25 Squadron, R.F.C., written by Lieutenant J. C. Whittaker, pilot. He arranged a board and notebook to strap on his knee, and wrote most of the lyrics, of which this is one, over the lines on patrol !   To the tune of " John Peel."*

AIRMEN'S OPENING CHORUS

D'ye ken 25 when the sun shines bright,
Going on bomb raids, their chief delight,
Showing the Huns the way to fight
And the way to Hell in the morning.

D'ye ken 25 with hearts so gay,
Waking up to find it's a nice " dud " day,
Doing sweet dam' all in their own sweet way,
Getting up jolly late in the morning.

The Orderly Officer's on the spot,
And whether it's " dud " or whether it's not,
He parades the batmen on the dot,
If he thinks there'll be flying in the morning.

D'ye ken the way that RAF-wires rust ?
And clean them you absolutely must,
Or the C.O.'s Flights kick up hell's own dust,
When they come round at ten in the morning.

D'ye *comprés* office in a quarter of an hour,
And if kept waiting the C.O. gets sour,
And if he is riled he will use his power,
To send you back to your unit in the morning.

D'ye *comprés* Observer on probagger,
Sunk in silent meditagger,
Searching hard for inspiragger,
How to get his " Brevet " in the morning.

Now we'll try to give you some idea,
Of the humours of war as they appear,
To us poor creatures stuck out here
Sing " Hail smiling morn " every morning.

Dating from 1916, 25 *Squadron, R.F.C., in which the appropriate commandment was quoted whenever suitable occasion offered. Of course, not a song but too characteristic of an R.F.C. mess to exclude.*

THE AIRMEN'S TEN COMMANDMENTS

1. I am the Lord Thy Flight Commander. Thou shalt have none other Flight Commander but me.

2. Thou shalt not take upon thyself any responsibility, neither in the office, nor on the aerodrome, nor in the Texas* for I thy Flight Commander am a jealous Flight Commander and visit the sins of the pilots upon the mechanics even to the first and second ack emma, who obey me and carry out my orders.

3. Thou shalt not take the name of thy Observer in vain, for thy Observer will not shoot any straighter if thou takest his name in vain.

4. Remember that thou keep holy " dud " days. In fine weather thou shalt work and aviate to thy heart's content ; but on " dud " days thou shalt clean no manner of RAF-wires, neither thou, nor thy rigger, nor thine engine men, nor thine Observer who is on probation.

5. Honour thy C.O. that thy days may be long on the aerodrome which thy Headquarters have given thee.

6. Thou shalt not crash thine Observer.

7. Thou shalt not seduce thy Flight Commander's landlady.

8. Thou shalt not pilfer thy neighbour's bombs.

9. Thou shalt not bear false witness after a bomb raid.

10. Thou shalt not covet the Recording Officer's job, nor his billet, nor his office, nor any cushy job that is his.

* The Texas Club

An R.F.C. air mechanics' song dating from early 1916, *written by Lieutenant J. C. Whittaker,* 25 *Squadron. To the tune of " The Rosary."*

THE AIR MECHANIC'S MOAN

The hours I spent with thee, dear bus,
Are as a string of plugs to me ;
I count the clearances in all your valves,
But you will miss—and still you miss.

Some pilots are—and some are not.
Some pilots can—and some cannot.
The engine's misfiring ! now w'ere o'er the line ;
I'm coming back : the fault's not mine.

And when the war is over,
I'm going back to Angleterre,
And then you'll hear La Belle France calling *moi*,
I don't think ; *Je ne pense pas.*

———

Sung in many R.F.C. messes in France. The lines are really much older and go back to an incident in India when a company of soldiers of a British regiment were decimated by typhus in a besieged camp. Sometimes sung to the air of Sir Arthur Sullivan's " The Lost Chord."

AN R.F.C. TOAST

We meet 'neath the sounding rafters,
  The walls all around us are bare ;
They echo the peals of laughter ;
  It seems that the dead are there.
    So, stand by your glasses steady,
      This world is a world of lies.
    Here's a toast to the dead already ;
      Hurrah for the next man who dies.

Cut off from the land that bore us,
  Betrayed by the land that we find,
The good men have gone before us,
  And only the dull left behind.
    So, stand by your glasses steady,
      This world is a web of lies,
    Then here's to the dead already ;
      And hurrah for the next man who dies.

A little ditty of the First World War expatiating on the advantages of civil service at Home compared with active service Overseas. There are more up-to-date versions—a fragment of one is sung in the closing scene of Terence Rattigan's play, Flare Path—*but I believe this is the earliest.* 1916.

I DON'T WANT TO JOIN THE AIR FORCE

I don't want to join the Air Force, I don't want to go to war I'd ra-ther stay at home A - round the streets to roam, Liv - ing on the earn - ings of a la - dy ty - pist. I don't want an Ar - chie where I sit down, I don't want my cra - nium shot a - way. I'd ra - ther stay in Eng-land, In mer - ry, mer - ry Eng-land, In the Air Board of - fice all the day.

I don't want to join the air force,
I don't want to go to war.
I'd rather stay at home
Around the streets to roam,
Living on the earnings of a lady typist.
I—don't want an Archie where I sit down,
I—don't want my cranium shot away.
I'd rather stay in England,
In merry, merry England,
In the Air Board Office all the day.

A CAPITAL BUS FOR A CROWD LIKE US

O ! a capital bus for a crowd like us was the old B.F.2B :
When once we got up we could sell a pup to anything we could see,
The leader we had was a hell of a lad
    For, according to what he'd say-ay-ay,
He could see the grimace on a pilot's face
    Ten thousand miles away.

      Then let the klaxon blow,
      A'roving we will go,
      We'll stay no more upon the floor, so take the chocks away !
      I'm off with my P.B.O., so let the Germans know
      That I'm out for some fun with a vertical Hun
      Ten thousand miles away.

A pilot we had was apparently mad, for he didn't know where to go,
He lost his way seven times a day, and relied on his P.B.O.
He would sail over Ghent with the best intent
    As happy as he could be-e-e-e,
And say with a grin, " My luck's well in,
    That must be I.A.D."

      The mess that we had was damnably bad, for we sat in the
         smoke all day :
      And some had been quick at the gas-mask trick,
      And others had passed away.
      The cook was a beast, and behaved like it, in spite of his hand-
         some pay-ay-ay,
      And his work was known by its smell alone
      Ten thousand miles away.

The recording bloke was a bit of a joke, though not such a bad old
    cuss ;
He is not to blame for his own pet name, but it's certainly hard on us;
The equipment man had a very good plan for combining work with
    pay-ay-ay,
For he went to Boulogne on stunts of his own
    Ten thousand times a day.

This song originated in the Royal Naval Air Service in 1916, *while serving in which Fred Godfrey wrote it—or, rather, wrote a version not intended for publication. Subsequently many variations of it were chorused in the R.A.F.*

until the present published words and music by Jimmy Hughes and Frank Lake appeared. It has always been the unofficial Trooping Song of the Royal Air Force.

THE R.A.F. TROOPING SONG—
BLESS 'EM ALL

There's ma - ny a troop-ship just leav - ing Bom -
- bay Bound for old Bligh - ty's shore,
Hea - vi - ly la - den with time ex - pired men
Bound for the land they a - dore. There's
ma - ny an air-man just fin - ished his time And
ma - ny a twerp sign - ing on They'll
get no pro - mo - tion This side of the o - cean, So
cheer up my lads, Bless 'em all.

CHORUS

Bless 'em all Bless 'em all The
long and the short and the tall. Bless all the

ser-geants and W—— O ones, Bless all the corporals and their blink-ing sons, For we're say-ing good-bye to 'em all___ As back to the bar-racks they crawl.___ You'll get no pro-mo-tion This side of the o-cean, So cheer up my lads, Bless 'em all.___

They say if you work hard you'll get better pay,
We've heard it all before.
Clean up your buttons and polish your boots,
Scrub out the barrack room floor.
There's many a rookie has taken it in,
Hook, line and sinker and all,
You'll get no promotion this side of the ocean,
So cheer up my lads, Bless 'Em All.

They say that the Sergeant's a very nice chap,
O what a tale to tell!
Ask him for leave on a Saturday night,
He'll pay your fare home as well.
There's many an airman has blighted his life
Thro' writing rude words on the wall,
You'll get no promotion this side of the ocean,
So cheer up my lads, Bless 'Em All.

They say that the Corp'ral will help you along,
O, what an awful crime!
Lend him your razor to clean up his chin,
He'll bring it back ev'ry time.
There's many a rookie has fell in the mud,
Thro' leaving his horse in the stall,
You'll get no promotion this side of the ocean,
So cheer up my lads, Bless 'Em All.

A song sung by 54 *Squadron, containing some excellent advice, and to the tune of " The Only, Only Way," from that typical-of-the-period musical comedy, " Tonight's the Night."*

THE ONLY WAY

If by some delightful chance,
When you're flying out in France,
Some old Boche machine you meet,
Very slow and obsolete,
Don't turn round to watch your tail,
Tricks like that are getting stale ;
Just put down your beastly nose,
And murmur, " Chaps, here goes ! "

Chorus :
It's the only, only way,
It's the only trick to play ;
He's the only Hun, you're the only Pup,
And he's only getting the wind right up,
So go on and do not stop
Till his tail's damn near your prop.
If he only crashes this side in flames,
Well, you'll only know they'll believe your claims—
 So keep him right
 In the Aldis sight—
It's the o-o-only way !

If on escort you should go
When the " Fees " are very slow,
While the Archies grumph and roar,
And Huns gather by the score :
If a nasty Hun should strive
On some poor F.E. to dive,
There's no choice at all, and so
Down your nose must go !

Chorus :
It's the only, only way,
It's the only trick to play,
Though your only gun will only fail,
And there's only six Boches on your tail,
And the F.E. shoots at you,
As we know they sometimes do—
Well, shoot him down instead of the Hun,
And you'll only say when the job is done,
 " Oh, poor old bean,
 Archie got him clean."
It's the o-o-only way !

A flying training song. Please note that in the R.F.C. " Hun " had two meanings—and the other one was " flying pupil " (he wrecked so many of our aircraft). This is the meaning we are concerned with here. To the tune of " Are You from Dixie? "

THE SONG OF THE HUN

" Say, Mister stranger, how do you do?
There's something I want to say to you :
That bus I see, what would it be?
Was it a triplane or an old 2E? "

" I'll tell you all that you want to know,
They sent me up on my first solo :
All went on grand, sir, I tried to land, sir,
Then unluckile-e-ee . . ."

Chorus :
We hit the ground once, I pulled the stick back,
Like my dear instructor taught me to do.
And then we rose—by gad, we rose up—
And the wind was rising up too !
I remembered that instructor said the nose down to stuff.
I looked around and said, " Oh, this is not good enough ;
I kept the stick back,
We hit the ground—*whack* !
Now I'm for trenches too ! "

————

Sung by air mechanics and others in the Royal Flying Corps. The reference to " my four " is to enlistment for four years or four years in reserve. An erroneous impression existed that on completion of this four years the ack emma would be able to return to civilian life whether the war was finished or not. To the tune of " There is a Happy Land."

THIS IS THE FLYING CORPS

This is the Flying Corps
So people say,
Where air mechanics lay the drains
For two bob a day.

O ! you should hear them sing,
" Roll on when my four is in,
Then back home my hook I'll sling,
And there I'll stay."

26

A songlet from about 1916-17, *having its own tune.*

LOOPING THE LOOP

Loop-ing the loop with Lu - cy Loo,

Looping the loop with Lu; —— Whirling and twirling the

whole day long, In a bus that's built for two, —— Then

up in the sky so high we fly, And then with a

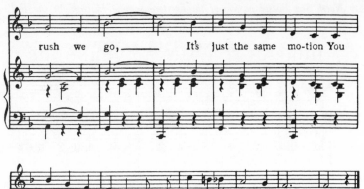

rush we go,_____ It's just the same mo-tion You

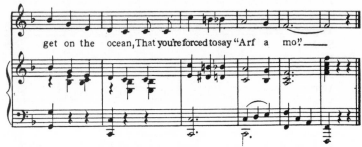

get on the ocean, That you're forced to say "Arf a mo."_____

Looping the loop with Lucy Loo,
Looping the loop with Lu ;
Whirling and twirling the whole day long,
In a bus that's built for two ;
Then up in the sky so high we fly,
And then with a rush we go.
It's just the same motion
You get on the ocean
That you're forced to say " 'Arf a mo."

———

Sung by 54 *Squadron to the tune of·* " *Sister Susie's Sewing Shirts for Soldiers.*"

R.F.C. ALLITERATIONS

Dirty Danny's digging deeper dug-outs,
Much deeper dug-outs dirty Danny dug to make a fug,
    One day he dug a topper,
    But the General came a cropper
In that damn, deeper, dirty, deeper, dug-out Danny dug.

Heavy-handed Hans flies Halberstadters,
In handy Halberstadters for a flight our Hans does start ;
    His Oberst says, " O dash it,
    For I fear that he will crash it,
See how heavy-handed Hans ham-handles handy Halberstadts !"

HURRAH FOR THE BOUNDING AIR

An aviator bold am I—
    Yo ho, my lads, Yo ho !
With joy I cleave the Western sky—
    Yo ho, my lads, Yo ho !
I love the roaring of the gale and hate the gentle breeze,
I hate a calm and placid day, but welcome storm-tossed seas.

Yo ho ! Yo ho !
So let the Tempest blow,
Hurrah, hurrah for the atmosphere,
Hurrah for the bounding air.
With a Yo-heave-ho for the bumps that throw
You almost anywhere.
I saw a submarine one day,
I thought it not quite safe to play,
So I dropped my bombs three miles away !
Hurrah for the bounding air.

On dud machines I always fly—
    Yo ho, my lads, Yo ho !
For then I know I can't get high—
    Yo ho, my lads, Yo ho !
For if I flew a new machine one day perhaps I'd meet
A Zeppelin or Gotha, and for that I'd have cold feet.

Yo ho ! Yo ho !
So let my bus be slow.
Hurrah, hurrah for the atmosphere,
Hurrah for the bounding air.
With a Yo-heave-ho for the bumps that throw
You almost anywhere.
On old B'E.s I hurl through space,
And hostile aeroplanes I chase,
But I know I haven't got their pace !
Hurrah for the bounding air.

I hate all forms of frightfulness—
    Yo ho, my lads, Yo ho !
I love the comfort of the Mess—
    Yo ho, my lads, Yo ho !
I love to sit in an easy chair before the blazing coal,
I much prefer my nice warm bed to the chilly Dawn Patrol.

Yo ho! Yo ho!
So let the others go.
Hurrah, hurrah for the atmosphere,
Hurrah for the bounding air,
With a Yo-heave-ho for the bumps that throw
You almost anywhere.
The honours list I read with zest,
I wish them all of luck, the best,
So long as I in peace can rest,
Hurrah for the bounding air!

---

*A pretty parody of a popular bass-baritone ballad, sung in R.F.C. messes.
Again the theme is death in a crash. To the tune of " Asleep in the Deep."*

STORMY THE NIGHT

Stormy the night and a lowering sky,
   Proudly the plane doth ride.
List how the passenger's startled cry
   Rings as he clutches the side.
There in his cockpit the pilot lays,
   Cursing his ballast who weakly prays.
Though death be near, he knows no fear,
   For at his side are a dozen beer.
     Chorus:
       Brightly the flares from the landing ground blaze
       Bidding us list to the hint it conveys.
       Pilot take care—pilot take care!
       Hundreds have crashed, so beware, beware!
       Many brave hearts have neglected their charts,
       So beware, beware!

What of the tempest the following morn?
   There is no trace or sign,
Save where the wreckage bestrews the corn
   Peacefully the sun doth shine.
But ere the wild raging storm did stop
   Two gallant airmen were caught on the hop,
No more to roam, afar from home,
   No more forced landings because of the Gnome.
       Brightly the flares from the landing ground blaze,
       Bidding us list to the hint it conveys.
       Pilot take care, pilot take care!
       Hundreds have crashed so beware, beware!
       Many brave hearts have been mixed with spare parts,
       So beware, beware!

Sung by 1 Squadron of the Australian Flying Corps in the Palestine Campaign 1916-17 to the air of Chopin's " Marche Funèbre"—this makes a beautiful dirge.

PUSHING

Where will we be in one hundred years from now?
Pushing up the daisies,
Pushing up the daisies,
Pushing up the daisies,
That's where we'll be in one hundred years from now.

2nd movement—
There let me be beside the river.
There will I rest for e'er and ever.
There will I be in one hundred years from now,
One hundred years from now.
Hundred years from now.
Years from now.
From now.
Now.

––––––

An amusing little song-parody of 1916-17 *about aero-engines. The sentiments expressed are the precise opposite of those, in truth, felt. " G " is pronounced hard as in " gong." Sung to the tune of " Show Me the Way To Go Home."*

I WANT A G-NÔME

I want a G-nôme,
Give me G-nôme.
I don't want a Monosoupape or Le Rhône,
I want a G-nôme

I want a G-nôme,
Give me a G-nôme.
Give me the splutt'ring, conking G-nôme,
I want a G-nôme.

Up, up in the sky,
Over the aerodrome,
Oh my! I do want to die.
I want a G-nôme.

32

This song-parody was published in Aeronautics *in* 1917, *by " G.R.S.,"*
and thereafter sung in the R.F.C. to the tune of the well-known ballad.

EXCELSIOR UP TO DATE

The shades of night were falling fast
As to the aerodrome there passed
A youth, with jaw set like a vice,
Who bore aloft this strange device :
                Keep Flying !

His brow was glad : his eyes were bright,
Reflected in the starry night !
And as he staggered to his bus
We heard him faintly whisper thus !
                Keep Flying !

Beware the Lewis gun that jambs !
Beware the shaky struts and cams !
The engine, too, is thick with rust."
" Oh, rats ! " the youth replied.   " I must—
                Keep Flying ! "

" Try not the flight ! " the sergeant pressed.
" 'Twill mean ' No flowers, by request,'
And currents roll both deep and wide ! "
But loud that clarion voice replied :
                " Keep Flying ! "

" Oh, stay ! " the Flight Commander said,
" The wine in mess flows good and red,
The sherry sparkles, rich and bright ! "
A voice replied, far up the height :
                " Keep Flying ! "

At break of day we started out
And scanned the heavens for this Scout.
And as we whistled through the air
We heard a dulcet voice declare :
                " Keep Flying ! "

There, in the tree-top, that young coon
Perched like a punctured kite balloon.
And when the ambulance drew nigh
We heard his last despairing cry :
                " Keep Flying ! "

WHEN THAT DAWN PATROL SETS OUT

When that Dawn Patrol sets out to cross the lines,
I'll be right there, I'll do my share,
When we see suspicious buses revving east.
We're far too low.   That's Von Bulow.
Albatri! Albatri! (*piano* : *bang*)
The beggar's on my tail,
I'm turning rather pale,
My bus seems like a snail.

As down I go : oh!
Why can't that damned Archie stop!
Gee! I've been and shot my prop!
Have a heart—have a heart,
For I'm on the early show.

When that Dawn Patrol gets over to Gontrode,
I'm with them still (against my will) ;
When we see some black and white ones underneath,
We've done it—once-too-often,
That's Richthofen!
Albatri! Albatri! (*bang*).

He's stalling up to me,
And shooting up at me!
Why can't the leader see the Huns below?   Oh!
Only one last thing I ask—
Where's that wretched brandy flask?
Have a heart—have a heart,
For we're on the early show.

THE BIRDMAN

I want to be an airman bold,
   To mingle with the stars,
To fly all weathers, hot and cold,
   To be a son of Mars.
I fear no Hun ; no, far or near,
   While my gun's mounted in the rear,
And I've a Vickers by my side,
   To be my escort and my guide.

Without chorus this parody of "The Wreck of the Hesperus" may be sung to the tune of "There is a green hill far away," but here it is set to the music of "Frankie and Johnnie"; a squadron song expounding upon the fateful shortcomings of an Air Mechanic Observer and how they led to—

THE WRECK OF THE OLD F.E.

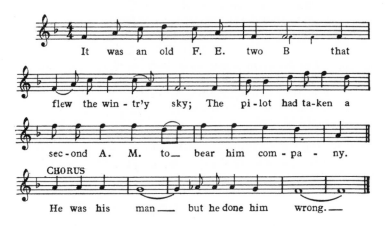

It was an old F. E. two B that flew the win-tr'y sky; The pi-lot had ta-ken a sec-ond A. M. to— bear him com-pa - ny.

CHORUS

He was his man — but he done him wrong. —

It was an old F.E.2B,
 That flew the wintry sky ;
The pilot had taken a second A.M.
 To bear him company.

  Chorus: He was his man, but he done him wrong.

Red were his eyes as the crimson rose,
 His nose as the dawn of day ;
His feet as cold as the mess-room stove
 As they ploughed their chilly way.

The skipper he sat in the pilot's seat,
 His heart was in his mouth,
As he watched how the veering wind did blow
 The clouds now west, now south.

Then up and spake the observer
 With a gesture of his hand,
" I'm hanged if I know where the hell we are,
 So hurry up and land."

" Last week the sky was full of planes,
 Today no planes we see."
But the pilot spat on his aneroid
 And a scornful laugh laughed he.

35

Higher and higher he climbed his bus,
  And looked for his escort bold ;
But they were down in the mess-room hut
  (If you wish the truth to be told).

Down came the storm and smote amain
  The F.E. in her strength ;
She shuddered and stalled like a frightened steed,
  Then dropped a cable's length.

" Lie down, lie down, my little A.M.,
  And do not tremble so ;
For I can weather the roughest gale
  That ever wind did blow."

" Oh, Captain ! I hear a pop, pop, pop ;
  Oh, say, what may it be? "
" It's a blasted Hun on my blinking tail " ;
  And he turned around to see.

" Oh, Captain ! I see two crosses black ;
  Oh, say, what may it be? "
" Grab hold of that Lewis and shoot, you fool,
  And don't stand talking to me."

" Oh, Captain ! I don't understand the gun,
  Oh, say, what shall I do? "
But the Captain's words were wafted back,
  And broke the prop in two.

Then down through the fleecy clouds below,
  The F.E. drifted fast ;
The observer thought of his future,
  And the pilot thought of his past.

But ever the fitful gusts between
  A sound—what can it be?
'Twas Archie paying his last respects
  To the wreck of the old F.E.

The trenches were right beneath her bows,
  She drifted a weary wreck,
And the Captain swore if he *did* get down,
  He'd break the blighter's neck.

She struck where the verdant waving grass
  Looked soft as a downy bed ;
But a couple of cows got in her way
  So she quietly stood on her head.

Full twenty yards across the ground
  The luckless pair were cast.
" I think I'll go," said the second A.M.,
  " The danger is not past."

At daybreak in a barren field,
  He still was running round ;
Whilst close behind the pilot came,
  Forever gaining ground.

The oil was frozen on his face,
  His mouth was full of sand,
But nearer came the avenger grim
  With the joystick in his hand.

Such was the wreck of the old F.E.
  In the land of rain and mud.
Lord ! save us all from such an A.M.,
  And make the weather dud.

———

Another squadron song deriding the productions of the Royal Aircraft Factory,
Farnborough. Probably earlier than 1917. *To the tune of* " *They Called*
it Dixie Land."

THEY CALLED THEM RAF 2Cs

Oh ! they found a bit of iron what
  Some bloke had thrown away,
And the " RAF " said, " This is just the thing
  We've sought for many a day."
They built a weird machine,
  The strangest engine ever seen,
And they'd quite forgotten that the thing was rotten,
  And they shoved it in a flying machine.
Then they ordered simply thousands more,
  And they sent them out to fight.
When the blokes who had to fly them swore,
  The " RAF " said, " They're all right ;
The bus is stable as can be ;
  We invented every bit of it ourselves, you see ! "
They were so darned slow, they wouldn't go,
  And they called them RAF 2Cs !

A song of the First World War, dating from early 1917, *when the German Fokker circuses were beating up the R.F.C. aeroplanes. Note: " R.A.F."* *means " Royal Aircraft Factory " which was at Farnborough, Hampshire,* *or alternatively " Royal Aircraft Factory Engine." To the tune of " Here We Go Gathering Nuts in May."*

THE RAGTIME AIRCRAFT BUILDERS

This they call a factory
a factory
a factory.
Its breadth and width is three by three,
It's called the R.A.F.

And here we build our aeroplanes,
a biplane,
and a monoplane.
With silly work we're nigh insane,
At the factory for aircraft.

Now two big sheets from mother's bed,
not sister's bed,
nor Lucy's bed.
Two big sheets from mother's bed,
They'll come in very handy.

Two big wheels from father's car,
father's car,
father's car,
Two big wheels from father's car,
They'll do very well.

Now this they call a fuselage,
a fuselage,
a fuselage,
You only call it fuselage
When you're in the know.

Next we have the longeron,
the longeron,
the one-plus-long.
Now that we have a longeron,
We'll stick it in the middle.

Now we'll shove the joystick in,
joystick in,
joystick in,
We'll just shove the joystick in
To make it look complete.

Next we'll have the motoro,
                the R.A.F.
            which will not go.
It's quite a puzzle to those in the know,
With all its idiosyncrasies.

We mustn't forget the old windstick,
                it goes alright
                without a flick,
But sometimes stops—then we look sick —
At five o'clock in the morning.

And now we've made an aeroplane
                a biplane?
                Or a monoplane?
We'll pack it up and send it by train,
So as not to spoil it.

            (*Over the lines*)
I think they're off their beastly rocker,
                perhaps they think
                it's a game of soccer.
They send me out against a Fokker,
They must have lost their valve-head.

            (*Two months later*)
And here I am in hospital,
                in hospital,
                Far from Pall Mall.
But when I come out I shall resign
My commission in the Army.

The Royal Aircraft Factory ("R.A.F.") was the butt of derisive humour in the R.F.C. This song was sung about the R.A.F. Engine to the tune of "Ten Little Nigger Boys." 1917.

ODE TO THE R.A.F. ENGINE

Eight lit-tle cyl-in-ders Sit-ting fac-ing heaven,

One blew its head off, Then there were seven.

Eight little cylinders sitting facing heaven,
One blew its head off—then there were seven.
Seven little cylinders used to playing tricks,
One warped its inlet valve—then there were six.
Six little cylinders working all alive,
One got a sooted plug—then there were five.
Five little cylinders working all the more,
One over-worked itself—then there were four.
Four little cylinders flying o'er the sea,
One shed a piston ring—then there were three.
Three little cylinders wond'ring what to do,
One over-oiled itself—then there were two.
Two little cylinders very nearly done,
One broke a valve stem—then there was one.
One little cylinder trying to pull round seven,
At length gave its efforts up and ascended into heaven.

From 22 Squadron, R.F.C., probably 1917, one of the many parodies to the tune of " Another Little Drink Wouldn't Do Us Any Harm ". The last line of each verse is repeated as chorus.

ANOTHER THOUSAND REVS

Oh there was a lit - tle hun, and he saw an aw - ful sight, A pa - trol of Twen - ty two sim - ply spoil - ing for a fight; So he shoved down his nose in a man - ner far from calm, And a - no - ther thou - sand revs would - n't do him an - y harm.

CHORUS

And a - no - ther thou - sand revs would - n't do him an - y harm.

Oh there was a little Hun, and he saw an awful sight,
A patrol of " 22 " simply spoiling for a fight ;
So he shoved down his nose in a manner far from calm,
And another thousand " revs " wouldn't do him any harm.

Now we had a little plan for shooting down the Hun ;
With a top Lewis gun we would have a lot of fun ;
But the sight of that gun simply filled them with alarm,
Though a burst in the tail wouldn't do them any harm.

Oh a pilot came to us who went out to learn the Lines,
And on his way back he didn't know the signs ;
He mistook for the Aerodrome a little French farm,
But the crash that he had didn't do him any harm.

Oh we had a P.B.O. who went out upon a job,
And the first Huns he met were the Comic Baron's* mob ;
So immediately he saw them he seized the pilot's arm
And said : " If we turned *West* it wouldn't do us any harm ".

Now there was a Bristol pilot, and he dived upon a Hun,
And he found when he was on it that he couldn't fire his gun ;
Then the Circus* dived upon him, to his horror and alarm,
Now a little nip of rum wouldn't do him any harm.

* Manfred Freiherr von Richthofen's squadron

Believed to have originated in 70 Squadron, R.F.C., this goes to the tune of " Oh Where Has my Little Dog Gone ?"   The last verse and chorus libel the Royal Naval Air Service, but pardonably—the Camel pilot had to escort the far superior DH4's.

SONG OF THE CAMEL PILOT

The Camel is a noble bird,
Complete with wings and hump,
It flies about like any scout
And then comes down with a bump.

> *Chorus :*   Oh where oh where have my two wheels gone ?
> Oh where oh where can they be ?
> They're not around upon the ground,
> They're up in the air don't you see ?

" Ve vos de German Flying Corps,
Ze RE8's ve strafe vell.
But ve don't like zese Camels any more
Since Hans and Conrad vos killed.

> *Chorus :*   " Oh vere oh vere has ze Camel gone ?
> Oh vere oh vere has it got ?
> Ze Albatros vent down in flames,
> Ze brutal Englisch did not."

The Navy went on a bombing show
To strafe the Hun on the ground,
They crossed the lines at a rate of knots
While we flew all around.

> *Chorus :*   Oh where oh where have the Navy gone ?
> Oh where oh where can they be ?
> They dropped their bombs from umpteen feet,
> And then went home in a pee.

A good song from American pilots of 184 *Squadron, R.F.C., France,* 1917-18.
*It has the same theme as that of " The Bold Aviator."   The fourth line in
the first verse is characteristic.   To the hymn tune " There Is A Better Land."*

THE LAST LAY OF THE SOPWITH CAMEL PILOT

Beside a Belgian 'staminet when the smoke had cleared away,
Beneath a busted Camel, its former pilot lay.
His throat was cut by the bracing wires, the tank had hit his head,
And coughing a shower of dental work, these parting words he said :

Oh, I'm go - ing to a bet - ter land, They
binge there ev - 'ry night, The cock-tails grow on
bush - es, So ev - 'ry - one stays tight. They've
torn up all the cal - en - dars They've bust - ed
all the clocks, And lit - tle drops of whis - ky Come
trick - ling through the rocks.

The pilot breathed these last few gasps before he passed away,
" I'll tell you how it happened—my flippers didn't stay,
The motor wouldn't hit at all, the struts were far too few,
A shot went through the gas tank, and let the gas leak through.

" Oh, I'm going to a better land, where the motors always run,
Where the eggnog grows on the eggplant, and pilots grow a bun.
They've got no Sops, they've got no Spads, they've got no Flaming,
     Fours,
And little frosted juleps are served at all the stores."

----

*" Ten Little Nigger Boys " has been parodied time and time again by
airmen.   This is one example, written in hospital April 1918 by Guy M.
Knocker, later Group Captain.   For others, see the second World War period.*

TEN LITTLE ALBATRI

Ten little Albatri flying on the line,
Three Camels met them,
Then there were nine.

Nine little Albatri thought they'd have a Hate,
One of them crossed the Lines,
Then there were eight.

Eight little Albatri flying close to Heaven,
Forgot about the Dolphin quite,
Then there were seven.

Seven little Albatri doing funny tricks,
One dived his wings off,
Then there were six.

Six little Albatri in a mighty dive,
One didn't see the ground,
Then there were five.

Five little Albatri took on the Flying Corps,
And it's not very wonderful,
That soon there were but four.

Four little Albatri out upon a spree,
One crashed on landing,
And so there were three.

Three little Albatri—a silly thing to do—
Attacked a Bristol Fighter,
Then there were two.

Two little Albatri flying all alone,
The silly fools collided,
Then there were none.

Sung by American pilots and observers in France to the tune of " When Johnny Comes Marching Home." 1917/18.

THERE WERE THREE HUNS

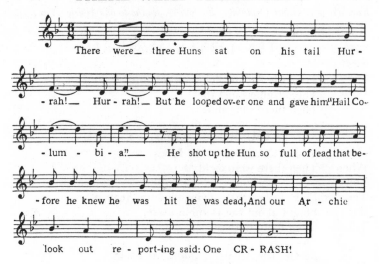

There were three Huns sat on his tail
Hurrah! Hurrah!
But he looped over one and gave him " Hail
Colum-bi-a."
He shot up the Hun so full of lead
That before he knew he was hit he was dead,
And our Archie lookout reporting said :
One!—CR-R-R-ASH!

46

This songlet tells how an Albatros Scout, seeking to bully some slow B.E.s, is overtaken and doomed by two fast-flying Sopwith Pups. Sung by 54 Squadron.

HUSH-A-BYE BABY

Hans vos mine name, and a pilot vos I,
Out mit Von Carl I vent for a fly ;
Pilots of Kultur ve vos, dere's no doubt,
Both of us flew in an Albatros scout.
Ve looked for B.E.s for to strafe mit our guns,
Ven last I saw Carl I knew he was dones,
For right on his tail there were two little Sops !
Oh, hush-a-bye baby on the tree-tops !

A nice little song about the P.B.O.=Poor bloody observer. He took very much of a back seat, yet his work was vital and he suffered hardships and dangers unknown to the pilot. The last verse is literally true: cases were not uncommon in 1914-18 of observer being thrown clean out of the aircraft through violent action by the pilot. O.P.=Observation Patrol. Sung to the tune of " A Bachelor Gay " from " The Maid of the Mountains."

YOU'RE ONLY A P.B.O.

When you get in the old machine to start on a damned O.P.
You cover yourself with tons of clothes and they're all of them N.B.G.
The pilot sits in the engine's fug, his body with heat aglow,
But you must stand in the back and cuss
Till the ice on your whiskers stalls the bus,
    You're only a P.B.O., oh pity the P.B.O.

Chorus:

At seventeen he's shooting rather badly at a Pfaltz of tender blue,
At fifteen thou. you see him point out sadly some Huns of different hue,
At ten or twelve you find him shooting madly at six or eight or more,
When he fancies he is past hope
Fires a long burst as a last hope,
And the Huns spin down on fire to the floor.

When you're doing an escort stunt and the Huns get on your tail
You fire and aim till you see 'em flame and down they go like hail.
Alas ! the pilot's jealous scorn is a thing we learn to know,
You may get umpteen Huns in flames,
Don't think that they'll believe your claims,
    You're only a P.B.O., yes, only a P.B.O.

Chorus :

At seventeen he's shooting rather badly. . .

We all of us know the case when the pilot came home alone,
No doubt it was only a slight mistake but his attitude's clearly shown,
He suddenly shoved his joystick down as far as it would go,
" Hello, you seem to have gone " he said.
" I fear you must be somewhat dead,
But you're merely a P.B.O., yes, merely a P.B.O."

Chorus :

At seventeen he's shooting rather badly. . .

Another song sung by the American pilots of 184 *Squadron, R.F.C.,* 1917-18.
To the tune of " John Brown's Body."

UP IN A SOP

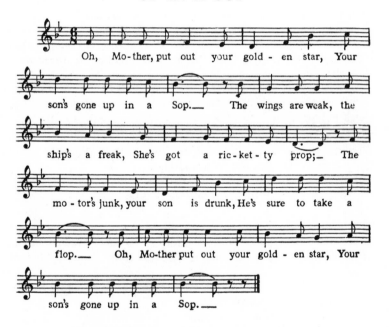

Oh Mother, put out your Golden Star,
Your son's gone up in a Sop.
The wings are weak, the ship's a freak,
She's got a ricketty prop ;
The motor's junk, your son is drunk,
He's sure to take a flop.
Oh, Mother, put out your Golden Star,
Your son's gone up in a Sop.

Dating from 1917, *this air-gunnery song alludes to the gun-firing through-propeller gear, early types of which were very faulty ; so " synchronised fire control " becomes, in the song, " syncopated fire control." Sung by* 54 *Squadron to the tune of " The Kipling Walk."*

THE SYNCOPATED FIRE CONTROL

In F.E.s you can sit at ease ;
The trigger squeeze, just as you please ;
Because you've got two guns
To bring down lots of Huns.
If a jamb you get, you need not fret ;
You've one gun yet and you can bet
You'll still bring down the Hun.
In single-seater tractor scouts, you're always on the hop,
You've a synchronising fire control, so that you won't hit your prop.
When you're out on a Sopwith Scout,
And your gun cuts out there is no doubt
You're absolutely done,
You're got stiff by the Hun.

Chorus :
Oh, the syncopated fire control,
Very fascinating on the whole ;
Something new is that the Lewis has got it now.
Vickers have done it since they first begun it.
Then you hear your gun shoot *Pop !—Pop !—Pop !*
Crash ! and you know you've gone and shot your prop.
It's a matter for some chatter *:*
We're up the pole—
Hang that syncopated fire control *!*

IN OTHER WORDS

I was fight-ing a Hun in the hey-day of youth Or per-haps 'twas at Nieu-port or Spad.___ I put in a burst at a mod-er-ate range And it did-n't seem an-y too bad.___ For he put down his

nose in a cu-ri-ous way, And as I

watched him I'm hap-py to say.

CHORUS

He des-cend-ed with un-par-al-leled ra-pid-i-ty, His ve-

-lo-ci-ty 'twould beat me to com-pute, I

speak with un-im-peach-a-ble ve-rae-i-ty, With

ev-i-dence com-plete and ob-so-lute. He

suf-fered from spon-ta-ne-ous com-bus-tion As to-

-wards ter-res-tial sanc-tu-ary he dashed, And

underwent complete disinte-gration, In other words— he crashed.

I was fighting a Hun in the heyday of youth
  Or perhaps 'twas a Nieuport or Spad.
I put in a burst at a moderate range
  And it didn't seem any too bad.
For he put down his nose in a curious way,
  And as I watched him I'm happy to say :

      He descended with unparalleled rapidity,
        His velocity 'twould beat me to compute,
      I speak with unimpeachable veracity,
        With evidence complete and absolute.
      He suffered from spontaneous combustion
        As towards terrestrial sanctuary he dashed,
      And underwent complete disintegration,
        In other words—he crashed !

I was telling the tale when a message came through
  To say 'twas a poor R.E.8.
The news somewhat dashed me, I rather supposed
  I was in for a bit of a hate.
The C.O. approached me, I felt rather weak,

  For his face went all mottled, and when he did speak :
      He straffed me with unmitigated violence,
        With wholly reprehensible abuse,
      His language in its blasphemous simplicity
        Was rather more exotic than abstruse,
      He mentioned that the height of his ambition
        Was to see your humble servant duly hung.
      I returned to Home Establishment next morning,
        In other words—was stung !

As a pilot in France I flew over the lines
  And there met an Albatros Scout.
It seemed that he saw me, or so I presumed—
  His manœuvre left small room for doubt.
For he sat on my tail without further delay,
  Of my subsequent actions I think I may say :

      My turns approximated to the vertical,
        I deemed it most judicious to proceed.
      I frequently gyrated on my axis,
        And attained colossal atmospheric speed.
      I descended with unparalleled momentum,
        My propeller's point of rupture I surpassed,
      And performed the most astounding evolutions,
        In other words—split-arsed !

I was testing a Camel on last Friday week,
  For the purpose of passing her out,
And before fifteen seconds of flight had elapsed
  I was filled with a horrible doubt,
As to whether intact I should land from my flight.
  I half thought I'd crash—and I half thought quite right :

      The machine it seemed to lack coagulation,
        The struts and sockets didn't rendezvous,
      The wings had lost their super-imposition,
        Their stagger and their incidental, too !
      The fuselage developed undulations,
        The circumjacent fabric came unstitched,
      Instanter was reduction to components,
        In other words—she's bitched !

---

*A song about the aerodrome at St. Omer, R.F.C. headquarters in France.
To the tune of " My Old Kentucky Home."*

OMER DROME

      I've got a windy feeling round my heart,
        And it's time that we went home,
      I've got a great big longing to depart
        Somewhere back to Omer Drome.
      Huns are diving at my tail,
      Wind up—Gee !—I've got a gale.
        Guns are jamming,
        Pilots damning,
      Archies bursting all around us.
        And observers say,
        " Ain't it time that we came down? "
        So won't you split-arse back
        Along the track
      To my dear old Omer Town?

MY OLD YELLOW JACKET

Wrap me up in my old yellow jacket,
The one in which I used to soar ;
to soar.

Give my helmet, my map and my goggles—
I feel once again as of yore ;
as of yore.

Fasten the jacket around me,
Lift me into my place ;
my place.

For ne'er shall ye say I'd the wind up,
I've still life enough for the pace ;
for the pace.

Wrap me up in my old yellow jacket,
Give me the joystick to hold ;
to hold.

Let me fly once again o'er the trench line—
Thus shall my exploits be told ;
be told.

Oh ! it's good to be in the old jacket,
To hear, " Switch off—petrol on, sir " ;
" petrol on."

To repeat once again the word " contact,"
To hear the old engine go whir-r-r-r ;
go whir-r-r-r.

Now we're off—o'er the line will we *allez*,
To strafe and to bomb is our aim ;
our aim.

To win or to lose in a combat—
The game must be played just the same ;
just the same.

Ah ! see that Hun there—in the sun, lad,
Give him a burst of the best ;
of the best.

Poop, poop, poop—he's returning our fire,
  I must split-arse and stunt round him, lest . . .
                              round him, lest.

God ! I'm hit, curse him—I feel so dizzy ;
  I'm sorry, old thing—it's my fault ;
                              my fault.

My hand or my eyes not so steady :
  I don't feel as well as I thought ;
                              as I thought.

Down, down, in a nose-dive they're spinning,
  Down from ten thousand to two ;
                              to two.

Very slowly the machine comes out level,
  The sands of life not yet run through ;
                              not run through.

By instinct his actions are guided,
  The machine flying homeward bound now ;
                              bound now.

Th' observer, a-sweat and a-tremble,
  Scarce knows what has happened—nor how ;
                              nor how.

He knows naught of the art of controlling
  An unstable bus in the air ;
                              in the air.

It's his first ascent into the heavens—
  Sure, 'tis an experience rare ;
                              very rare.

Dazed—yet alive—he is landing :
  Blood from his scalp surges down ;
                              from his crown.

He moves not as they rush towards him,
  Ere then—his brave spirit has flown ;
                              has flown.

They laid him in his old yellow jacket,
  In peace ; and his spirit may soar—
                              may soar.

Far above, where the Huns cease from troubling,
  And Lewis guns rattle no more ;
                              no more.

An outstanding song that originated, about 1915, *among squadrons of the Royal Naval Air Service with the British Expeditionary Force in France. There were R.F.C. versions of it, but it is essentially a naval airman's ditty —note " make and mend " in the sixth verse. It was later sung in various versions in messes at home and overseas through the peace years. It recounts the exploits of a bold young pilot from the time he gets up in the morning for his early* (sic) *patrol to the time he celebrates his safe return in an Amiens café. Sung to the tune of " The Key Hole in the Door."*

I LEFT THE MESS-ROOM EARLY

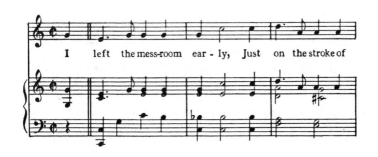

I left the mess-room ear - ly, Just on the stroke of

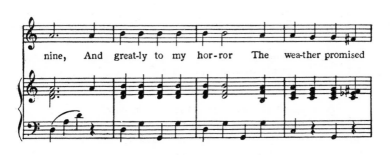

nine, And great-ly to my hor-ror The wea-ther promised

fine. I strolled down to the hangars, Their regions to ex-

I left the mess-room early, just on the stroke of nine,
And greatly to my horror the weather promised fine.
I strolled down to the hangars, their regions to explore,
And found my bus all ready, outside the hangar door.

I thought I'd try my engine to see what it would do,
The counter showed eight-fifty revs, the cylinders were blue,
The damn thing missed, say twenty times, which made me hold my
    breath,
As I climbed into the atmosphere to juggle there with death.

At last I reached four thousand feet and met the old F.E.s.
The morning air was very cold, which made my pecker freeze.
Just then we crossed the German lines, close to old Bapaume,
And as we saw the Archies burst we thought of Home Sweet Home.

The R.E.s they went westward, close followed by the Pup,
And by the time we reached Cambrai we had the wind right up.

Then turning once again for home my hopes were no avail,
For there were twenty Albatros a-sitting on my tail.

I went split-arse for glory, those beggars to avoid,
And when they saw my caperings those Huns were overjoyed ;
They emptied twenty pans or more right at my blooming head,
They fired some high explosives and a ton or two of lead.

At last we crossed the lines, once more at will to roam ;
We're tickled absolutely pink—we cannot find our home,
We land all over Western France, men everywhere they send
To work all through the dreary night, and dream of make and mend.

But safely at the 'drome once more, we feel quite gay and bright,
We'll take a car to Amiens and have dinner there tonight,
We'll swank along the boulevards and meet the girls of France :
To hell with the Army Medical !—we'll take our ruddy chance.

Additional verses:

Now talking of reconnaissance, I think you will agree,
The best machine for this good work is hardly Number 3.
And though we do our best to please and earn the major's thanks,
For all the ruddy good we do we might as well fly tanks.

Now we have got a rest camp just east of old Bapaume,
We thought it was a lovely spot, just like our home, sweet home.
Old Casey went out there one day, he thought it a good bid,
But the damned old Hun was active and I'll tell you what he did :

Old Casey just had dinner and climbed right into bed,
The bombs were dropping thick and fast around his weary head.
They shook the poor lad to the core, and he was scared pea-green,
When a fifteen-inch came over and removed the old latrine.

Monday is the guest-night of Navy Number 3,
Last Monday we were awfully pleased to see the R.F.C.
But when they introduced the game of old man Cardinal Puff,
They shortly got the Navy tight and soon things waxed quite rough.

SO EARLY IN THE MORNING

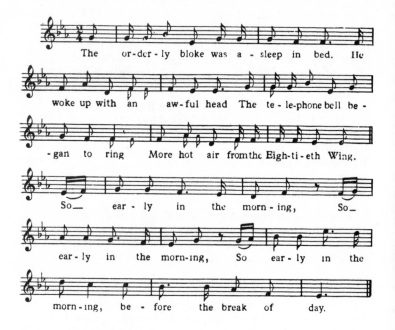

The or-der-ly bloke was a-sleep in bed. He woke up with an aw-ful head The te-le-phone bell be-gan to ring More hot air from the Eigh-ti-eth Wing. So— ear-ly in the morn-ing, So— ear-ly in the morn-ing, So ear-ly in the morn-ing, be-fore the break of day.

The orderly officer said, " Who's that? "
The Wing replied, " There's a Halberstadt
Over Albert, so they say,
Go and drive the blighter away."

So six unfortunate sleepy heads
Known as pilots left their beds,
The Flight Commander wiped his eyes,
And led his formation into the skies.

The patrol hadn't been gone five minutes, I'm sure,
When 80th Wing rang up once more :
" It isn't a Hun : the patrol must stop,
It's only an old two-seater Sop."

The morning mists began to rise
Until they filled the wintry skies.
The patrol should all have been back by nine.
At eleven o'clock there was no sign.

Then the squadron commander began to swear,
" Chaps," he said, " Oh dear, oh dear !
What has happened?   I'd like to know."
Then a message came through for our C.O.

" Archie's down by Albert way,
Tommy's crashed in a field, they say,
As for the others you can guess their plight,
It looks as though you've lost your Flight."

And now my story's nearly done,
And, as you see, there was no Hun.
The moral of it's perfectly clear,
We must have very much less *hot air*—
        So early in the morning,
        So early in the morning,
        So early in the morning,
        Before the break of day.

Sung by R.F.C. squadrons to the tune of the un-Hunnische " Mountains of Mourne." 1917-18.

TWO HUNNISCHE AIRMEN

Two Hunnische airmen were Adolf and me,
A pilot was I, an observer was he
And we used to spot for the Artillery,
As we sailed through the skies in an old L.V.G.
One day unexpectedly out of the sun
A big Bristol came with a big Vickers gun,
And after ten minutes of furious strife,
With a yell poor old Adolf departed this life.

On came the big Bristol, his gun spitting lead,
And after a while I got shot through the head ;
I never cried out, but just smiled instead,
For a curious feeling told me I was dead.
And now we sit up in the Heavens above,
Our heads are in halos, our hearts full of love,
For though they shot down poor old Adolf and me,
Here's jolly good luck to the old R.F.C.

Sung by flying training cadets in Canada in 1917 and 1918, almost in a monotone, as a march.

HEAVEN OR HELL

Do you ev - er think as a hearse goes by That it won't be long until you and I Go roll-ing by in a nice new shirt, And then they lay us right un - der the dirt. And the worms crawl out and the

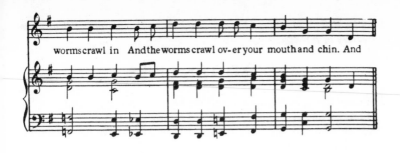

worms crawl in And the worms crawl ov-er your mouth and chin. And

as for your soul no man can tell Whether it goes to Heaven or Hell.

Do you ever think
As a hearse goes by
That it won't be long
Until you and I
Go rolling by
In a nice new shirt,
And then they lay us
Right under the dirt.

And the worms crawl out
And the worms crawl in
And the worms crawl over
Your mouth and chin.

And as for your soul
No man can tell
Whether it goes
To Heaven or Hell.

Sung by R.F.C. squadrons, France, 1917-18, to the tune of " I'll be off to Tipperary in the Morning."

OVER THE LINES

We were flying in formation and we kept our ruddy station,
　Though the wind was trying hard to sweep the sky.
And we watched the puffs of powder, heard the Archies booming
　　louder
And we didn't need to stop to reason why.

With the German lines below us, and a gale that seemed to throw us
　Into nowhere, as it would a schoolboy's kite,
We went skimming through the ether always keeping close together
And we felt the joy of battle grip us tight.

Then from out of the horizon which we kept our eager eyes on
　Swept the Fokkers in their deadly fan-wise dash.
Soon the Vickers guns were cracking and a couple started backing,
　Whilst a third was sent down in a flaming flash.

How we blessed our Bristol Fighters, as we closed in with the blighters
　And we zoomed and banked and raced them through the air.
We abandoned our formation, but we won the situation,
　Won it easily, with four machines to spare.

Then Archie burst around us, and the beggar nearly found us,
　But we dived towards our lines without delay,
And we finished gay and merry on a binge of gin and sherry,
　For we knew we'd lived to see another day.

———

A parody sung by R.F.C. pilots at mess parties 1917-18, to the popular song of the same name.

EVERY LITTLE WHILE

Every little while I crash a Camel, ·
Every little while I hit a tree ;
I'm always stalling—I'm always falling,
Because I want to fly a posh S.E.
Every little while my engine's conking,
Every little while I catch on fire.
All the time I've got my switch up
I've always got the wind up.
Every, every, every little while.

Fragment truthfully expressing feelings of war-weary pilots. 1917-18.

WINGS OF AN AVRO

Another concert party song of the Royal Flying Corps, France, 1917-18. *The R.E.8 was a two-seater fighter, more affectionately known as the " Harry Tate." A typical R.F.C. song-parody, with a crack at the conscientious objector in the last verse characteristic of the day. The last line of each verse is repeated as chorus. To the tune of " Another little Drink wouldn't do us any Harm."*

ANOTHER UNDERCARRIAGE WOULDN'T DO US ANY HARM

Oh, there was a little pilot and he flew an R.E.8.,
    He tried to make a landing but he flattened out too late.
The observer told the pilot in a voice of grave alarm,
    That another undercarriage wouldn't do us any harm.

Now there was an air mechanic and he over-stayed his pass,
    They tell me that the reason was a little blue-eyed lass.
Next day the C.O. said, in a manner sweet and calm,
    " Oh fourteen days' C.B. will not do you any harm."

Another air mechanic once was swinging on a prop ;
    He didn't know the switch was on—it caught him on the hop.
As the pilot stopped the engine, he muttered in alarm—
    " Another new ack emma wouldn't do us any harm."

Now there was a little French girl and she lived not far from here,
    She sold some liquid stuff that she said was lager beer.
But one night a sergeant heard her singing out this psalm—
    " Anozzer pail of vatter vill not do it any harm."

They tell us that at home there are fellows called C.O.s,
    Who object to straffing Huns and to striking any blows.
They prefer to stay in Dartmoor and admire its rural charm :
    Well, we think a damn good hiding wouldn't do *them* any harm.

A Royal Flying Corps concert party song-parody of 1917-18. *It tells of the perils that besought the slow-moving B.E.2, used for artillery observation, reconnaissance and bombing, often at the mercy of the German single-seater fighter unless escorted over enemy lines by one of our own scouts. The B.E.2 was introduced* 1916, *the F.E. (two-seater fighter) at the same time. The Sopwith Pup was later. To the tune of the song of the same name from the musical play " The Arcadians."*

MY MOTTER

I fly along on an old B.E.
   It isn't fast enough for me.
So when a little red Hun I see,
   I get in a nose dive.

I've gotter Motter—Keep on our side of the Line.
   If you go East by " You-know " Wood,
You'll get a bullet where no one should.
   The scouts may come (although the chance is a slim one) ;
I always say as I look up—
   " Perhaps that blighter's a Sopwith Pup,
   It's a small cross but a black one ! "

Each time I go up I meet a Hun ;
   Sometimes the odds are ten to one.
I simply whistle and cock my gun :
   I'm horribly reckless.

I've gotter Motter—Bolt when the Huns are in sight.
   Though you dodge and try to hide,
Every cloud has a Hun inside.
   The scouts may come (although the chance is a slim one);
I always say as I look up—
   " Perhaps that blighter's a Sopwith Pup,
   But I'm sure that old cross is a black one."

I had to go on photography,
   My escort was an old F.E.
Did he come over the Line with me?
   No—not bally likely.

But I had to do it. I did it almost in a trance.
   Though you think the Hun is dud,
You still hit the earth with a nasty thud.
   Now I've no more of this pitiful tale to tell you,
I still fly along on my old B.E.,
   Doing my best for the powers that be.
It's a short life but a gay one !

WE HAVEN'T GOT A HOPE IN THE MORNING

So I went to the sheds and examined my gun,
Then my engine I tried to run,
And the revs that it gave were a thousand and one
'Cos it hadn't got a hope in the morning.

We were escorting Twenty-two,
Hadn't a notion what to do,
So we shot down a Hun and an F.E. too!
'Cos they hadn't got a hope in the morning.

We went to Cambrai, all in vain.
The F.E.'s said, " We must explain,
Our camera's broke—we must do it again ! "
Oh, we haven't got a hope in the morning !

A bomber squadron song of 1917-18 *sung to the tune of* " *I Want To Go To Bye-Bye To Rest My Weary Head.*"

I WANT TO GO TO ESSEN

The Kaiser has seen a new kind of machine,
   Known as 9a's, known as 9a's,
To Mannheim they've been and they've upset his spleen,
   On some fine days, on some fine days.
But though Mannheim has tickled our keen appetite,
There's another Rhine town that was just out of sight—

   I want to go to Essen to lay my little egg,
      The Kaiser believes that it's out of my reach,
   Somebody's pulling his leg.
      And when I've been to Essen and called on Fraulein Krupp,
   My good old 9a can get back all the way,
      And the Kaiser will have the wind right up—right up.

So to Essen we'll go with a hell of a bombing formation—formation.
And from a great height we will drop a great weight of damnation
   —of damnation.
We'll drop a great weight of explosive on Fritz,
We'll blow all his principal shell-works to bits.

A squadron song, 1917-18, *which deals with the niceties of landing a D.H.9a. To the tune of* " *A Bachelor Gay* " *from* " *The Maid of the Mountains.*"

IF YOU WANT TO REMAIN INSIDE

When you're flying the old " Nine A" on a bumpy, windy day,
And your engine begins to splutter out and you think you have lost
   your way,
Be careful to keep your head to wind if you want to reduce your glide,
And side-slip over a down-wind fence,
If you want to remain inside your field,
If you want to remain inside, you want to remain inside.
Chorus:
At eighty-five you head her in so nicely, a glide you should not
   exceed ;
At seventy-five you flatten out precisely, and still you've got lots of
   speed.
At sixty-five you pull the stick back gently and put her on the floor.
But at fifty you'll be stalling,
And you'll realise you're falling,
And you'll crash her as she's never crashed before.

THE 100 SQUADRON LAMENT

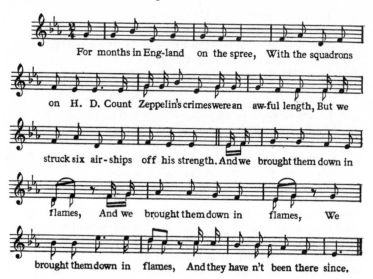

For months in Eng-land on the spree, With the squadrons
on H. D. Count Zeppelin's crimes were an aw-ful length, But we
struck six air-ships off his strength. And we brought them down in
flames, And we brought them down in flames, We
brought them down in flames, And they have n't been there since.

Then some brass hat at Adastra House
Tried his best to start a grouse,
To form " One Hundred " for overseas
He picked his men from the best H.D.'s.

> And they sent us out to France,
> And they sent us out to France,
> And they sent us out to France,
> To show them how to bomb.

We landed on the Western Front,
From Isel le Hameau was our first stunt,
And we soon ken from Jerry's moans
That he didn't like the aeros with the skull-and-cross-bones.

> For they blew up all his railways,
> For they blew up all his railways,
> For they blew up all his railways,
> And ammunition dumps.

Our pilots got well known round there,
So they moved us up to a place called Aire.
And we bombed his dromes till the Hun wished he
Could run across the Major they called Christie.

70

We wrote off his best drome,
We wrote off his best drome,
We wrote off his best drome,
And also the Menin Road.

Then Jerry, just to show his spite,
Bombed London with his planes at night.
The people said, " You silly clowns,
Why not go and bomb his towns ? "

     So they pushed us off to Ochey,
     So they pushed us off to Ochey,
     So they pushed us off to Ochey,
     To get square with the Hun.

Well, Jerry must have thought the same,
And he tried his best to stop the game.
We all remember that fine night
That brought the squadron their first fright.

     For he tried to wipe out Ochey,
     For he tried to wipe out Ochey,
     For he tried to wipe out Ochey,
     But the café stands there yet.

The wind-up there no man could stick,
And everyone paraded sick.
Then someone said t'would be the goods
To move up further in the woods.

     And everyone was happy,
     And everyone was happy,
     And everyone was happy,
     For there was rest, sweet rest.

When we got rid of our F.E.'s,
He got to work with twin H.P.'s,
And Jerry said (by what we hear)
That the only one he had to fear—

     Was good old Hundred Squadron,
     Was good old Hundred Squadron,
     Was good old Hundred Squadron,
     We hope to meet again.

A song of 55 Squadron, about 1918, sung to the tune of " Riding Down to Bangor." See also " A Song of 55 Squadron."

SING A SONG OF AIRCRAFT

Sing a song of aircraft used in the Great War.
Can you beat the record of the D.H.4?
Eighteen months on service and still going strong,
She may see the war out, if it's not too long.

Sing a song of engines, we use a Rolls-Royce,
Thank your stars, ye pilots, let your hearts rejoice.
You have the " 8 Eagle," horse-power three-fifty,
Lucky that it's not " Puma B.H.P."

Sing a song of Pilots from the Pilots' Pool,
Were it not for this war they would be at school ;
For more information youth at all times yearns,
Flying in formation here each pilot learns.

Sing a song of crashes on the aerodrome,
Think of all the hot air that there is at home,
But on Active Service it's another thing,
" Ack Eff double something," send it to the Wing.

Sing a song of squadrons, there's only one—our own,
When the war is over then the truth is known,
All the raids on Hunland surely will derive
Fame for the old squadron, No. 55.

The song of 54 Squadron which, in the First World War, was probably as well known as any for the songs its officers and men invented and sang. To the tune of " We've Come Up From Somerset."

SONG OF 54 SQUADRON

Oh ! We came out from Birmingham
    To see the great big war.
There was Oxo right chock full of fight
    And Nobby out for gore.
Archie shot at us " gr-r-umph ! umph ! "
    And blacked the sky so blue,
When right up flew a Halberstadt
    And said, " And vitch vos you? "

Chorus :   Oh, we've come up from Fifty-four,
        We're the Sopwith Pups, you know,
        And wherever you dirty swine may be
        The Sopwith Pups will go.
        And if you want a proper scrap,
        Don't chase 2C's any more ;
        For we'll come up and do the job,
        Because we're Fifty-four !

A two-seater looked at Oxo,
    And " Vot vas you? " he said ;
And Oxo blushed quite red with rage
    And shot the blighter dead.
Then we found some Hun balloonists
    Behind old Vendhuille Town ;
The Huns seemed keen to pull it in,
    And so we helped it down.

Then the Hun, he looked down on Peronne,
    From which he'd run away,
And Struggy, seeing seven there,
    Cried, " Splendid ! chaps, Hooray !
Although there's only four of us,
    You've got to fight, you see."
And so they went right into them—
    By gad ! They brought down three !

A lovely squadron song with excellent chorus. Once again the theme is the dreadful causes and consequences of the fatal crash. In this song there is much vocal by-play in the chorus lines within the verses—thus, " beyond belief" sung very expressively—and the whole done throughout with mock tragedy. The chorus lines are indicated by italics. From 1917.

WHICH HE'LL NEVER DO NO MORE

He was div - ing at the Hun   At two hun - dred miles an hour, When his wing tore off like a leaf.   They found him in the wreck (with his hand up-on the throttle) He was butchered be-yond be -

74

75

He was diving at the Hun
At two hundred miles an hour,
When his wing tore off like a leaf.
They found him in the wreck (*with his hand upon the throttle*),
He was butchered beyond belief.

Beyond belief—(*beyond belief*)
Beyond belief—(*beyond belief*)
He was butchered beyond belief.
He was diving at the Hun
(*Which he'll never do no more*)
'*Cos he's butchered beyond belief.*

He was driving through the sleet
At a bare two hundred feet,
With a compass that wouldn't stay still.
They found him in the wreck (*with his hand upon the throttle*),
For he'd buried his nose in a hill.

In a hill—(*in a hill*)
In a hill—(*in a hill*)
For he'd buried his nose in a hill.
He was driving through the sleet
(*Which he'll never do no more*)
'*Cos he's buried his nose in a hill.*

He was coming in to land
When his kite got out of hand,
And he spun where he shouldn't have done.
They found him in the wreck (*with his hand upon the throttle*)
And a mother now mourns for her son.

For her son—(*very sad*)
For her son—(*very sad*)
Oh, a mother now mourns for her son.
He was coming in to land
(*Which he'll never do no more*)
For a mother now mourns for her son.

A song of 110 *Bomber Squadron, Independent Air Force,* 1918, *sung to the tune of* " *Dixie Land.*"

BETTENCOURT

When the Boche was getting jumpy in the towns along the Rhine,
With the Handleys out at night time, and by day the D.H.9.
Then the Independent Air Force thought that things were getting
 slow,
And they really must do something, just to liven up the show.

So they found a spot for an aerodrome,
And they called it Bettencourt,
And they put up hangars round about,
And prepared the place for war.
And in the space of forty winks
They produced a crowd of Chinks,
And it wouldn't have been so ruddy
If it hadn't have been so muddy
And they'd put more cinder on the floor.
They erected stores and workshops,
And they did the thing in style,
They protected all their buildings
With revetments by the mile.
And when the place was nearly done
They brought along the finest bombing squadron, barring none
They made it twice as nice as Paradise,
And they called it Bettencourt.

The words of this song were written on April 1, 1918, the birthday of the Royal Air Force. It was afterwards set to music by R. H. Cort at the Apprentices School at Halton, and included in the comic opera "Time Flies," produced at that station in April, 1928. By A. C. Kermode.

A NEW TOAST

As we'll all ad-mit, the Roy-al Na-vy is the fin-est in the world: Far north and south, on ev-'ry sea The white en-sign is un-furl'd: And as for our gal-lant sol-dier boys, None bold-er than they of

course:___ But here's to the best that our

King em-ploys, To the men of the Royal Air Force.

CHORUS

So here's to those who fly, Wher-ev - er they may

be: To the ar-mies of the sky. Guard-ing land and

sea: For the land is wide and the sea is deep, But the air is_ larg-er still. So all to-night ere you fall a-sleep, To the brim your glass-es fill. And drink with me, This toast en-dorse: To the of-fi-cers and men, To the of-fi-cers and men of the Royal Air Force.

As we'll all admit, the Royal Navy is the finest in the world.
Far North and South, on every sea, the White Ensign is unfurled,
And as for our gallant soldier boys, none bolder than they, of course ;
But here's to the best that our King employs,
To the men of the Royal Air Force.

Chorus: So here's to those who fly, wherever they may be ;
To the armies of the sky, guarding land and sea :
For the land is wide and the sea is deep,
But the air is larger still ;
So all tonight ere you fall asleep,
To the brim your glasses fill.
And drink with me, this toast endorse,
" To the Officers and Men,
To the Officers and Men of the Royal Air Force."

To those who man the swift seaplanes, skimming lightly o'er the
foam ;
To the pilots of the aeroplanes who guard our hearth and guard
our home ;
To the stately silver airship's crew keeping watch o'er ships and coast;
To the parachutists, brave though few,
Come join in a right good toast.

To those who build our aeroplanes with delicate touch and skill,
To the aircraftmen who patch the planes, and the tanks with petrol
fill ;
Come raise your cups and drink with me, for each is doing his share ;
To win for Britain, who rules the sea,
The Mastery of the Air.

A nice parody of " I am the Ruler of the Queen's Navee," from Gilbert and Sullivan's " H.M.S. Pinafore." 1918.

NOW I'M A GENERAL AT THE MINISTRY

When I was a boy I went to war
As an air mechanic in the Flying Corps.
I dished out dope, and I swung the prop,
And I polished up my talents in the fitters' shop ;
And I did my work so carefully
That now I'm a General at the Ministry.

As an air mechanic I made such a name,
A sergeant-major I soon became,
I wore a tunic and Sam Browne belt,
And my presence on parade was most acutely felt.
My presence was felt so overwhelmingly
That now I'm a General at the Ministry.

As a sergeant-major I made such a hit
That I demanded further scope to do my bit,
Of my lofty ways there was never any doubt
And they sent me up in a Nieuport Scout,
I flew so well over land and sea
That now I'm a General at the Ministry.

I flew in France with such amazing zest
That the King grew tired of adorning my chest,
People boosted McCudden, Bishop and Ball,
But readily agreed that I out-soared them all.
My merits were declared so overwhelmingly
That now I'm a General at the Ministry.

So mechanics all, wherever you be,
If you want to climb to the top of the tree,
If your soul isn't fettered to a pail of dope,
Just take my tip—there's always hope,
Be smart in the Strand at saluting me
And *you'll* be Generals at the Ministry.

From the song-book of 22 Squadron, dating from the Armistice but written as though forty years later. A parody of W. S. Gilbert's Bab Ballad, " The Yarn of the Nancy Bell."

THE YARN OF "TWENTY-TWO"

Being told by the sole survivor of this Squadron in the World War which raged in the early days of this century, to wit one Shanks, a man of feeble intellect, who, 'tis said, has been known to stretch the long-bow to great lengths. Albeit as the doddering old man told it to me, so I pass it on to you.

'Twas on a 'drome within our shore
    From here to there but a span,
That I found with a ring-sight and Lewis gun,
    An Elderly Aerial Man.

His hair was woolly, his beard was long,
    And woolly and long was he ;
And I heard this wight on the 'drome recite
    In a singular minor key :

" Oh I am Observer, and Pilot bold,
    And C.O. of ' Twenty-two,'
And the E.O. tight, and the R.O. bright,
    And the Captain staunch and true."

And he shook his fists, and he tore his hair,
    Till I really felt afraid,
For I couldn't help thinking that the man had been drinking,
    And so I simply said :

" Oh, Elderly Man, 'tis little I know
    Of the duties of Men of the Air,
But I'll eat my hand if I understand
    How you be as you declare."

And he looked at the sky, begged a fill and a match,
    Put his Lewis gun under his arm,
Got a light, murmured thanks, said " My name is Shanks,"
    And he spun this pitiful yarn :—

'Twas with good old Squadron " Twenty-two "
    That we fought in the last great war,
And many were killed, and their places were filled,
    And still we cried for more.

Thus nine years passed, and in the tenth
  Things had come to a terrible plight :
We called for men, but couldn't get them—
  Not a man was there left to fight.

We couldn't say pax to the ravaging Hun,
  So we sent up the ground personnel,
And still we kept flying and still we kept dying—
  'Tis a heart-rending tale to tell.

And pretty nigh all of them were killed,
  Yes, many a hundred o'soul,
Till only seven of the Squadron's men
  Said " Here " to the muster-roll.

There was me, an Observer, and Pilot bold,
  And the C.O. of " Twenty-two,"
And the E.O. tight, and the R.O. bright,
  And a Captain staunch and true.

The Captain true and Observer bold,
  Were next on the list to go ;
Then we spun at roulette, and I won, you bet,
  For who went with our dear C.O.

They never came back, so the Pilot said :
  " It's one of you two with me."
So a penny I tossed, and the E.O. lost,
  Thus deciding which it should be.

So I made up the logs, and I tested the guns,
  And commanded " Twenty-two."
I checked stores to a thing, sent returns to the Wing,
  But my Squadron never flew.

So I started a prop, and climbed into the 'bus,
  And I thought " Where'er will it cease ?"
Then fears I did flout, flew the thing as a Scout,
  And lo ! *on a sudden came—PEACE !*

Now I never laugh, and I never smile,
  And never a trick I play ;
But I sit and croak, and a single joke,
  I have—which is to say :—

" Oh, I am Observer and Pilot bold,
   And C.O. of ' Twenty-two ',
And the E.O. tight, and the R.O. bright,
   And the Captain staunch and true."

E.O.—Equipment Officer. R.O.—Recording Officer (Adjutant).
Shanks—Lieutenant Shanks, Squadron Equipment Officer 1917-18.

Captain Norman Macmillan, in his book Out of the Blue, *relates how a number of officers returned very happily early one morning from a fancy dress party. One of them decided to " shoot up " the C.O.'s residence, in the course of which he crashed on the aerodrome. Still fancily attired, his companions later danced around the aircraft singing this songlet, as the dazed pilot emerged from the wreckage. 1918. To the tune of " Ring-a-Roses."*

POOR OLD PILOT

Poor old pi - lot's dead,— Poor old pi - lot's dead.— He's killed him - self, he's killed him - self, Poor old pi - lot's dead.

Poor old pilot's dead,
Poor old pilot's dead.
He's killed himself,
He's killed himself,
Poor old pilot's dead.

This toast in 1918 was annexed from the Royal Irish Constabulary by 141 Squadron stationed at the time in Ireland: thence it spread to others and, though the R.I.C. is long since dead, its toast lives on. It is proposed by each diner who, if he fails to sing it or makes a mistake, has to provide another bottle. At the command Drink *the company stands and obeys. Each member of the company takes his turn, starting on the left of the chairman.*

A SQUADRON TOAST

I, friend, drink to thee, friend,
   As my friend has drunk to me ;
And you, friend, will drink to your friend
   As I, friend, drink to thee.

   And the more we drink together, friends,
     The merrier we'll be ;
   And the more we drink together, friends,
     The merrier we'll be.

DRINK !

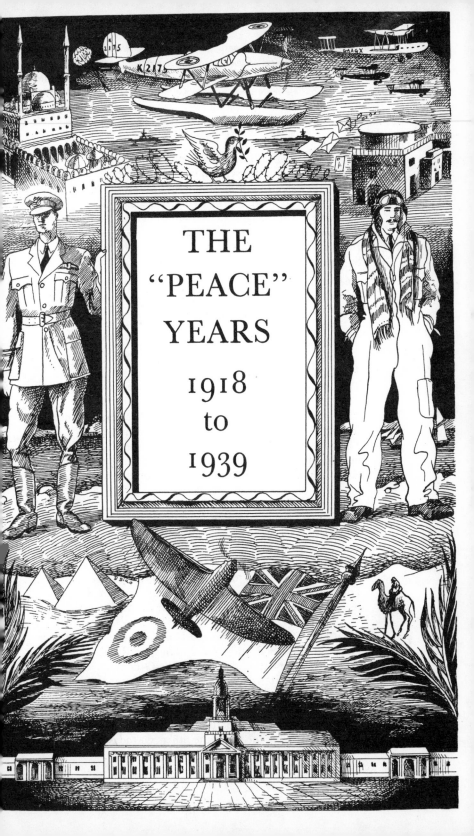

THE "PEACE" YEARS

1918 to 1939

A bomber squadron song of the post-Armistice period, recording the amusement caused by the blue uniform of the new Royal Air Force (1918-1919), a little squadron history, reference to 55's companions, 99, 104 and 110 squadrons, and to the peace-time work of mail-carrying. To the tune of " The 5.15."

A SONG OF 55 SQUADRON

Look at all those fellows clad in pale blue:
Aren't they awful dressy, don't you like the hue?
Surely they should not be wandering round the land,
Members of some uninterned Hungarian band.
They are not musicians, nor commissionaires—
You mustn't judge a person by the dress he wears.
I asked one for a taxi, and he feigned that he was deaf,
So I guess he is a member of the R.A.F.

   Chorus:

      Fifty-five!   Won't you join this chorus?
      Fifty-five!   Come on, shout it loud!
      Fifty-five!   None is classed before us,
      Best of all the squadrons in the old R.A.F. crowd!

The visit paid to Darmstadt made the Huns quite cross:
They nearly got a bull's-eye on the Ducal Schloss.
The Kaiser, too, was angry, remembering the time
They missed him by the hour when they bombed Mannheim.
But had he only waited he might have really won
The title of All Highest, and he might have hit the sun.
But the Horrid Hohenzollern knows one thing now quite well,
His direction is not skyward, but the shortest road to hell!

Think of all the bomb raids done by Fifty-five,
Isn't it a marvel that any Hun's alive?
Think of all the misses, think also of the hits,
Think of the munition train they blew to bits.
Give a thought to Frankfurt, to Bonn give one or two,
And Treves, Coblenz, and Durren, and don't forget Karlsruhe.
Think of Ludwigshafen, where poison-gas was made,
In volume only rivalled by the hot air from Brigade.

What about a word now for old Ninety-nine?
They did jolly good raids round about the Rhine.
Also we must mention Squadron One-O-Four,
They were too at Azelot and helped to win the war.
At Bettencourt were stationed Squadron One-One-O—
But this is all a memory, it is so long ago.
" Sic transit " for the squadrons which now have passed away.
" Air transit " for the mails the others do today.

A post-Armistice song of the winter of 1918. *To the tune of " John Brown's Body."*

A TWENTY-FOUR SQUADRON SONG

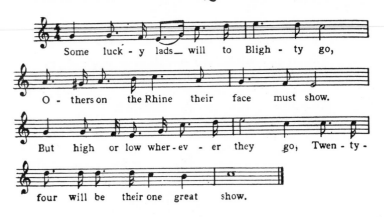

Some luck-y lads— will to Bligh-ty go,

O-thers on the Rhine their face must show.

But high or low wher-ev-er they go, Twen-ty-

four will be their one great show.

> Some lucky lads will to Blighty go,
> Others on the Rhine their face must show.
> But high or low, wherever they go,
> Twenty-four will be their one great show.

The flying training song of a pupil on his first cross-country flight, to the tune of " Un Peu d'Amour " (" Just a Little Love—a Little Kiss.")

JUST A LITTLE OIL

> Can you please direct me to my aerodrome?
> I have lost my way—my water too.
> But before you put me on my way for home,
> There are several things I want from you.
>
> Just a little oil—a drop or two,
> Just some gasolene to see me through,
> Hands that lightly swing my prop and shove me,
> How I know the Duty Flight will love me!
>
> Three times now I've tried to get to Spittlegate,
> Still I'm wandering all round Salisbury Plain,
> While the weather's lifting—while the engine lasts,
> Hasten, I beseech you, once again—
>
> Just a little oil—a drop or two,
> Just some gasolene to see me through,
> Hands that lightly swing my prop and shove me,
> How I know the Duty Flight will love me!

Song of 28 Squadron, North-west Frontier of India, from 1919 *onwards. It was sung until the Bristol Fighter went out of service. To the tune of the ballad, An Old-Fashioned Town." See " That Old-Fashioned Avro of Mine (page* 130*) and a variant of the second World War, " Old-Fashioned Wimpey," 70 Squadron, all songs of affection.*

AN OLD FASHIONED BRISTOL

There's an old-fashioned Bristol
  With old-fashioned planes,
    And a fabric all tattered and torn ;
An old-fashioned engine that starts with a roar
  And a sound like a thousand tin cans.
Tho' she won't loop nor spin
'Cos she's nearly done in,
    Still there's something that makes her divine :
For she's quite safe and sound
'Cos she won't leave the ground !
    Will that old-fashioned Bristol of mine.

Coda :
Twenty-eight, in dear old Twenty-eight,
Finest Squadron in the Force just let me state ;
We're always there when there is something to do,
And our pilots are the finest boys that ever flew.
Twenty-eight, in dear old Twenty-eight,
Always in the running for some fun ;
Those days of jollity will live in our memory,
When our days in Twenty-eight are done.

———

An old song (though not quite so old as the dates suggest !) of the Central Flying School, Upavon, on Salisbury Plain.

IN THE MIDDLE OF SALISBURY PLAIN-O !

In 1892 I found myself with nothing to do,
I found myself with nothing to do—
      In the middle of Salisbury Plain-O !

Chorus: Patsie atsie ooral-i-ay, patsie atsie ooral-i-ay,
        Patsie atsie ooral-i-ay—
        In the middle of Salisbury Plain-O !

So in 1893 I went and joined the R.F.C.,
I went and joined the R.F.C.—
 In the middle of Salisbury Plain-O!

In 1894 I opened my engine out with a roar,
I taxied about all over the floor—
 In the middle of Salisbury Plain-O!

In 1895 I was thankful to find myself alive,
I was thankful to find myself alive—
 In the middle of Salisbury Plain-O!

For in 1896 I found myself in a dreadful fix,
I crashed by Rumpety into sticks—
 In the middle of Salisbury Plain-O!

In 1897 I tried to climb right up to heaven,
Oh, I tried to zoom right up to the moon—
 From the Middle of Salisbury Plain-O!

But in 1898 I nearly met with an awful fate,
I side-slipped right from the Golden Gate—
 To the middle of Salisbury Plain-O!

Oh, in 1900 and 1 and 4 the R.F.C. went off to war,
The R.F.C. went off to war—
 From the middle of Salisbury Plain-O!

In 1900 and 1 and 5 the Fokker mono began to dive,
And aerobatics began to thrive—
 In the middle of Salisbury Plain-O!

So in 1900 and 1 and 6 we found ourselves in a hell of a fix,
So we brought out a thing called a D.H.6.
 In the middle of Salisbury Plain-O!

In 1900 and 1 and 8—that was the end of the War so great,
And that was the end of the R.E.8—
 In the middle of Salisbury Plain-O!

From airmen's messes in Iraq in the 1920's : sung in canteens and such resorts.   To the tune of an old Cockney song of the same name.

HOLD YOUR ROW

Way out in I – raq a fort – night I'd been When
I got a mess – age from my lit – tle queen, Say – ing
how she'd got mar – ried a fort – night a – go, Five—
years is a long time to wait don't you know Hold your
row,_____ what' cher say,_____ We can beat all the

S.   p's   who   come   down   our   way.   Hold   your   row.

Way out in Iraq a fortnight I'd been
When I got a message from my little queen,
Saying how she'd got married a fortnight ago,
Five years is a long time to wait, don't you know.

    Chorus :   Hold your row, what'cher say,
               We can beat all the S.P.s who come down our way,
               Hold your row, what'cher say,
               We can beat all the S.P.'s who come down our way.

So I took to the bottle, I took to the glass,
And I stuck to MacEwan's as long as it last,
Till one night in Baghdad the cops picked up me,
And the lousy old C.O. said " Fourteen C.C."
    Chorus

Now Baghdad's a city of wonderful sights,
The girls in the restaurants they all dress in tights,
And they drink ginger ale while you pay for champagne,
Then they say " Not tonight, Dear, I'll see you again."
    Chorus

Fourteen more days and the Boat will be here,
Fourteen more days and we'll leave Basra Pier.
And the finest of sights in the whole of Iraq
Is from the stern of a Trooper that's not coming back.
    Chorus

One of the best-known overseas songs which was a development of a parody by Lieutenant J. C. Whittaker, R.F.C., in 1916 on much the same theme. R.A.F. Station, Shaibah, Iraq, was established in the 1920's on the Persian Gulf, in the Shatt-el-Arab, or delta of the Tigris and Euphrates. " Those Shaibah Blues " is an expression that came to be synonymous with homesickness among airmen. Sung especially by 70, 84 and other Middle Eastern squadrons. The verse goes to the tune of " A Little Bit of Heaven " but the chorus is an original dirge.

THOSE SHAIBAH BLUES

A little piece of *mhutti* fell from out the sky one day,
It fell into the Persian Gulf not many miles away,
And when Lord Trenchard saw it there it looked so bleak and bare ;
He said, " That's what we're looking for—we'll put our Air Force
 there."
So—they sent out river gun-boats, armoured cars and A.H.Q.,
And then they put our squadron right in that *maknoon* blue.
Oh, *peechi*, I'll be going to a land that's far remote,
Until that day you'll hear me say,
" Roll on that *maknoon* boat ! "

Chorus:

>   I've got those Shaibah Blues, Shaibah Blues,
>   I'm fed up, and I'm tired out, and I'm old.
>   Oh, I've been sitting here for close upon two year,
>   And I wish I were in my coffin underground.
>   I've tried to learn the lingo, but it's fairly got my goat,
>   The only thing that I can say's " Roll on that *maknoon* boat ! "
>   I've got those Shaibah Blues, Shaibah Blues,
>   I'm fed up, and I'm tired out, and I'm old.

Mhutti =Mud, muck.   *Peechi* =presently, soon.   *Maknoon* =mad, silly.

Between 1920 *and* 1925 *R.A.F. squadrons were on continuous operations in Waziristan, N.W. Frontier of India, yet were not officially " On active Service." They flew Bristol Fighters and DH9A's. The operations were described as police work to preserve peace. Bombing villages, cattle and tribesmen was a dirty job, especially in aircraft over mountainous terrain. The piece below by R. H. Peel, though not written for singing, is nevertheless very much a song of that time and place.*

THE "PEACE" OF WAZIRISTAN

" Oh Big 9A ! Oh Big 9A !
What are *you* doing Razmak way ?
Why these bombs, this pomp of war ?
Surely your home's in Risalpur ?"

" Pomp be damned ! You make me laugh,
There ain't no pomp in this small strafe :
I'm bombing hell from a local Khan
To keep the Peace of Waziristan !"

" Oh smart Brisfit ! Oh smart Brisfit !
What are *you* doing in fighting kit ?"

" I'm praying hard to avoid a ' konk '
On offensive patrol from a sink called Tonk,
Down the gorges and up Splitoi
Sniped to blazes, but Attaboy !
They called it war on the banks of the Marne
But bless you ! it's Peace in Waziristan !"

" If they ask me, what shall I say
To the folks at home, back England way ?"

" Don't you worry—there's naught to tell
'Cept work and fly and bomb like hell—
With hills above and hills below
And rocks to pile where the hills won't go—
Nice soft sitting for those who crash.
But ' War ' you call it?—Don't talk trash !
War's a rumour—war's a yarn—
This is the Peace of Waziristan."

Sung at the Royal Air Force Cadet College, Cranwell, 1924, to the tune of " The Lincolnshire Poacher."

NOW I'M AN AC/3

I joined the R.A.F. as an aircrafthand as good as good could be,
But after a month my Conduct Sheet was one of the sights to see ;
It was full of fines and days in Quod my Leader gave to me,
I was five times up to the Wing Commo and twice to the A.O.C.
So—I started again as an A/C2, and now I'm an A/C3.

A fragment sung irreverently by airmen at inspections by the Air Officer Commanding to the tune of the Royal Air Force ." General Salute."

A.O.C's INSPECTION

Parade, Parade, Attention !
　Here comes the Air Vice Marshal !
Stand at ease, you silly lot of dopes,
　It's only the Sanitary Corporal.

A good chorus song from the early 1920's, *or possibly earlier. It cocks a snook at the dignity of Station Commander, Flight Commander and Warrant Officer (or Sergeant Major, as he is still called colloquially).*

OFFICERS OF "A" FLIGHT

Officers of "A" Flight
Sitting on the hangar wall,
Watching the Flight Commander
Doing sweet damn-all.
Chorus: When they are promoted
What will they do?
Same as the Flight Commander,
Sweet damn-all too!

Officers of " B " Flight
Standing at the tarmac edge,
Watching the Flight Commander
Landing through the hedge.
When they are promoted
What will they do?
Same as the Flight Commander,
Drink too much too!

Officers of " C " Flight
Standing at the office door,
Watching the Flight Commander
Pass out on the floor.
When they are promoted
What will they do?
Same as the Flight Commander,
And pass out too!

Airmen of the squadron
Slopin' round the place,
Watching the Sergeant Major's
Great big beery face.
When they are promoted
What will they do?
Same as the Sergeant Major,
Drink too much too!

Officers of the station
Scarcely make the grade,
Watching the Station Master
Swaying on parade.
When they are promoted
What will they do?
Same as the Station Master,
Drink too much too!

Sung at flying training schools in the early 1920*'s to the hymn tune " What a Friend we have in Jesus."*

FLYING TRAINING

When this rotten term is over,
Oh, how happy I shall be!
No more sitting on the tarmac,
No more circuiting for me.
No more taking off and landing,
No more waiting on the grass,
And we'll kiss the Flight Commander
As he hands us our last pass.

From the Royal Air Force Cadet College, Cranwell, Lincolnshire, this parody of the W. S. Gilbert lyric was sung in a concert party show, Christmas, 1925, and is a good example of the way the Service twists tunes and words to its own requirements of the moment. In fact, the song is an excellent caricature of the cadet of the period. The college was inaugurated in 1920, the cradle of the R.A.F. Sung to the tune of " A Most Intense Young Man," from " Patience."

THE SONG OF THE CADET

My style you'll quickly get—
An every-day Cadet,
The usual type
With moustache and pipe,
And occasional five bob bet.
My talk's of engine shop
And how I made her hop,
My favourite hobby,
Evading the bobby,
In especial the local cop.

A most intense young man,
An ever so fit young man.
But ne'er a gyration,
Nor examination,
Easily beat young man.

First Termer:

A bowler hat young man,
A crammer's pup young man,
A Mother's delectable,
Father's respectable,
Junior Term young man.
A sober keen young man,
A forming-fours young man.
An alpha plus essay
On d'Urbeville Tessy,
Foot-well-on-the-rung young man.

A premier school young man,
A varsity type young man,
Considerably shaken,
Home-sick and forsaken,
Yellowish beak young man.

Second Termer:

A Second Term young man,
A growing-up young man.

A budding line-shooter,
With A.J.S. Scooter,
Imbibing at half a can ;
Who thinks first termers worms,
And only thinks in terms
Of motor bike fuel
And solo and dual
And heterodynes and therms.

A wireless-set young man,
A crystal-set young man,
A most irritating
With damned oscillating,
Unlicensed set young man.

Third Termer:

When I go in the air
Instructors all declare,
With groaning and chaffing
And cursing and straffing,
At the things that I do and dare.
I fly with graceful ease
Three feet above the trees.
And little I reck
To fly into the deck—
More work for the keen A/C's.

A motor bike young man,
A golfing type young man,
With wonderful stockings
With intricate clockings,
Plus seven or eight young man.

Fourth Termer:

An N.C.O. young man,
Conceive me if you can.
I fly every type
Though, indeed, on the Snipe
I'm but one of the also ran.
I never lose my prop,
If e'er my engine pop,
With a delicate grace
I dip earthwards and place
My machine on a youthful crop.

A responsible type young man,
A torchlight tattoo young man.
A dashing young sergeant
Abounding in argent,
A ten-bob-a-day young man.

A Royal Air Force song sung by most squadrons since 1925. *In* 1921 *the British Government handed over responsibility for military control of the mandated territory of Iraq from the Army to the Royal Air Force (8 squadrons). In* 1924 *an anti-Arab and anti-British insurrection started among the local Kurds, centring in Sulaimaniya, near the Persian border,* 150 *miles Northeast of Baghdad. It was led by Sheikh Mahmoud, against whom the squadrons operated on and off till* 1931. *In its original version the song told of the agonising things that would happen to the crew of aircraft that force-landed in the hostile territory around Sul.*

THE BALLAD OF SULAIMAN

In the year an - no do - mi - ni One - nine - two -
- four 'Twas just out - side Sul - ai - man there start - ed a
war. H. - Q. got ex - cit - ed And sent down to

"Bert" To pull op-er-a-tions staff Out of the dirt.

CHORUS

No bombs at all, No bombs at all, If our

en-gines cut out we'll have no bombs at all.

In the year anno domini one-nine-two-four,
'Twas just outside Sulaiman there started a war.
H.Q. got excited and sent down to " Bert "
To pull operations staff out of the dirt.

Chorus:　No bombs at all, no bombs at all,
　　　　If our engines cut out we'll have no bombs at all.

There once were two pilots set out to bomb Sul—
Their bombs were alright but their tanks were half full.
Then from the back came the agonised call,
" If our engines cut out we'll have no bombs at all."

Chorus:　No bombs at all, no bombs at all,
　　　　If our engines cut out we'll have no bombs at all.

'Twas just over Sul that both engines cut out ;
And again from the back came the agonised shout,
" If we land to the east of the Basrean Pass,
Might as well throw that Lewis gun out on the grass."

Chorus: No bombs at all, no bombs at all,
             If our engines cut out we'll have no bombs at all.

They looked o'er the side and 'twas quite plain to see,
Sheikh Mahmoud and his tribesmen were seated at tea,
A'sitting around 'midst their herds and the rocks
Discussing spring fashions in stockings and socks.

Chorus: No bombs at all, no bombs at all,
             If our engines cut out we'll have no bombs at all.

They landed and ran like the chaff 'fore the wind,
With a bowie knife flashing six inches behind,
They knew they were in for some terrible thrills,
So they hitched up their pants and they ran for the hills.

Chorus: No bombs at all, no bombs at all,
             If our engines cut out we'll have no bombs at all.

St. Peter reclined on a large fleecy cloud
When the Orderly Angel came fluttering around—
" Excuse me, St. Peter, 'tis quite plain to me
That here is a signal which you ought to see—
It's by W.T., and it's marked with a ' P,'
Addressed to ' St. Peter, repeat Holy Three.'
Sender's name it is ' Air '—today's date—and to say
That an old Rolls-Royce Vernon is coming this way."

Chorus: For they've no bombs at all, no bombs at all,
             Their engines cut out and they've no bombs at all.

They landed at last and were full of good cheer,
St. Peter said, " Chaps, shall we split the odd beer? "
The pilots replied in a voice loud and shrill,
" We thank you, St. Peter, we think that we will."

Chorus: For we've no bombs at all, no bombs at all,
             'Cos our engines cut out and we've no bombs at all.

The moral of this it is quite plain to see :
Look after your fuel tanks where'er you may be,
And when 'midst the Arabs and Kurds you must roam
If you *must* employ petrol don't leave it at home !

Last line sung in falsetto.

Another typical airman's song from Middle Eastern stations in the Peace Years. A Two-Five-Two is, of course, a Charge Sheet. To the tune of "Casey Jones."

ON A TWO-FIVE-TWO

The day you go to Hai-fa you will rue,— There's bags of bull and red— tape— too And if you don't do the things you ought to do— You'll find your-self up-on a Two-five-two

CHORUS

On a Two-five-two, A Two-five-two,— You'll find your-self— up-on a Two-five-two

The day you go to Haifa you will rue,
There's bags and bags of bull and red tape too.
And if you don't do the things you're told to do
You'll find yourself upon a Two-Five-Two.

Chorus : On a Two-Five-Two, a Two-Five-Two,
　　　　　You'll find yourself upon a Two-Five-Two.

One day into Haifa you will barge
And find yourself upon a charge,
They'll whip you up before the A.O.C.
And they'll dip you from a Corporal to an L.A.C.

Chorus : Oh an L.A.C. !　Oh an L.A.C. !
　　　　　They'll dip you from a Corporal to an L.A.C.

One day the Sergeant Major he says to me,
" My lad your cap ain't T.D.C.*
And if you want to see the Promised Land
Oh you'll straighten up the cap badge with the mohair band."

Chorus : " The mohair band, the mohair band,
　　　　　Oh you'll straighten up the cap badge with the mohair
　　　　　band."

Now my warning's ended, I don't know any more,
So just sing this chorus, just once more,
I could sing about the Squadron but that'd never do,
I'd land myself for sure upon a Two-Five-Two.

Chorus : A Two-Five-Two, a Two-Five-Two,
　　　　　I'd land myself for sure upon a Two-Five-Two.

* T.D.C. – Top Dead Centre

A trifle from Airmen's messes in the Middle East around 1930.

AC.2's ARE COMMON

Slowly and with deep feeling

A C 2's are com - mon, A C 1's are rare, L A C's are plen - ti - ful, you'll meet them a - ny - where, Cor - porals they are stin - kers Ser - geants they are too; But the Sta - tion War - rant Of - fi - cer is a bas - tard through and through.

A.C.2's are common,
A.C.1's are rare,
L.A.C.'s are plentiful,
You'll meet them anywhere.

Corporals they are stinkers,
Sergeants they are too.
But the Station Warrant Officer
Is a bastard through and through.

———————

*Sung at the Royal Air Force Cadet College, Cranwell, 1924, to the tune of
" The Arrow and the Song."*

THE AVRO AND THE SONG

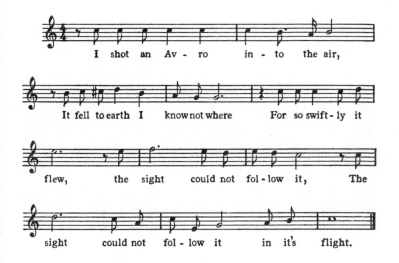

I shot an Avro into the air,
    It fell to earth I know not where,
For so swiftly it flew, the sight
    Could not follow it in its flight.

I breathed a prayer into the air
    And shot to earth I know not where.
My parachute so tight and strong,
    I followed as it dragged along.

Long, long afterwards by an oak
I found that Avro badly broke.
And the prayer, from beginning to end,
On my trial was the pilot's friend.

———————

Written by A. C. Kermode, with music by R. H. Cort, for the comic opera "Flat Out" produced at R.A.F. Station, Halton, by aircraft apprentices in April, 1930, and reproduced from "The Halton Song Book."

THE FITTERS' SONG

CHORUS

We are the Fit-ters, Fit-ters A. E. are we, are we,

Ar-mour-ers and Fitters D. P. Fitters of ev-'ry kind and degree

We are the Fitters. There are o-ther kinds of mi-nor trades,

Rig-gers of mul - ti - fa - ri - ous grades,

Cop - per-smiths of va-rious shades, But we are the Fit-ters

Fit-ters A. E. are we, are we, Ar-mourers and Fitters D. P.

Fitters of ev - 'ry kind and de-gree, We are the Fitters,

Rig - gers are on - ly a kind of dis - ease,

Cop - per - smiths! go down on your knees,

Fine

Clear the gang-way if you please, For we are the Fit-ters.

Fine

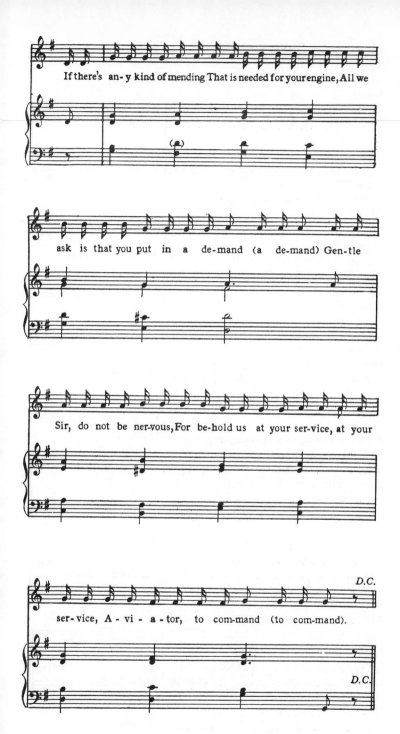

If there's an-y kind of mending That is needed for your engine, All we

ask is that you put in a de-mand (a de-mand) Gen-tle

Sir, do not be ner-vous, For be-hold us at your ser-vice, at your

ser-vice, A - vi - a - tor, to com-mand (to com-mand).

D.C.

If there is any kind of mending
That is needed for your engine,
All we ask is that you put in a demand (a demand).
Gentle Sir, do not be nervous,
For behold us at your service,
At your service, Aviator, to command (to command).

Chorus:
We are the Fitters, Fitters A.E., are we, are we,
Armourers and Fitters D.P.
Fitters of every kind and degree.
We are the Fitters.

There are other kinds of minor trades,
Riggers of multifarious grades,
Coppersmiths of various shades,
But we are the Fitters,
Fitters A.E. are we, are we,
Armourers and Fitters D.P.
Fitters of every kind and degree,
We are the Fitters.
Riggers are only a kind of disease,
Coppersmiths! go down on your knees,
Clear the gangway if you please,
For we are the Fitters.

If your crankshaft needs aligning,
Or your bearings need relining,
And connecting rods are creaking in their cranks (in their cranks).
If your engine needs decoking,
If it's popping back or smoking,
We gen'rally can cure its little pranks (little pranks).

You will never find a better,
For to tune your carburetter,
We can change its merry note in half a shake (half a shake),
And to make the job completo
We will time the old magneto,
And guarantee to break the make and break (make and break).

If your little end is binding,
Or your cylinder needs grinding,
Or the valve is feeling sticky in its guide (in its guide),
We can bore or grind or lap it,
We can bend it, scrape it, scrap it,
Or tap it with its tappet from inside (from inside).

If we hear the fatal hissing,
Of a sparking plug that's missing,
We are not averse to scrounging at a pinch (at a pinch).
And we're usually able,
With a suitable log table,
To calculate the thous. in half an inch (half an inch).

The riddles of expansion
We refuse to take a chance on,
So we keep a stock of clearances in store (in store),
Behold us the disciples
Of Herr Otto and his cycles,
And fitters from the case unto the core (to the core).

———————

In the 1920's this song came to be sung in R.A.F. messes overseas when an airman was about to leave on the boat for Home. It was sung to actions, sometimes to a ceremony. The posted airman stood on the mess floor (or table) attired in his tropical kit, discarding each item of clothing at the appropriate verse until he was finally stripped. Chorus lines are in italics.

SONG OF THE SHIRT

This old coat of mine,
The inside's fairly clean.
But the outside has seen some dirty weather.

So I'll cast this coat away
Until the blooming Day.
Roll on the ship that takes me Home.

This old collar of mine,
The inside's fairly clean.
But the outside has seen some dirty weather.

So I'll cast this collar away
Until the blooming Day.
Roll on the ship that takes me Home.

This old tie of mine,
The inside's fairly clean.
But the outside has seen some dirty weather.

So I'll cast this tie away
Until the blooming Day.
Roll on the ship that takes me Home.

This old shirt of mine,
The inside's fairly clean.
But the outside has seen some dirty weather.

So I'll cast this shirt away
Until the blooming Day.
Roll on the ship that takes me Home.

And so on until the strip-tease is completed.

A troopship song sung by squadrons afloat and in the East. It has the same theme as dozens of other overseas songs—Roll on the Boat for Home, sometimes abbreviated to R.O.T.B. It originated in Iraq, but was amended to fit the country in which it was sung. Its chorus is that of " Those Shaibah Blues," Shaibah blues having come to mean overseas-weariness generally rather than with blues peculiar to R.A.F. Station, Shaibah, Persian Gulf. The S.S. Somersetshire, owned by the Bibby Line, was the queen of all R.A.F. troopships.

SHIRE, SHIRE, SOMERSETSHIRE

We're leaving Khartoum on the cattle saloon,
We're travelling by night and by day,
We're passing Kasfret and we've nothing to eat
For we've thrown all our rations away.

Shire,   shire,   Som-er-set—shire, The   skip-per looks

on her with pride.___ He'd have some-one struck if he

saw an-y muck On the side of the Som-er-set-shire.

This is my sto-ry,___ This is my

song,___ I've been in I -

Shire, Shire, Somersetshire,
The Skipper looks on her with pride.
He'd have someone struck
If he saw any muck
On the side of the Somersetshire.
This is my story, this is my song,
I've been in Iraq too bloody long.
So roll on the Nelson, the Rodney, the Hood,
For this ruddy place is no ruddy good.

I've got those Shaibah Blues, Shaibah Blues,
I'm fed up, and I'm tired out and I'm old.
Oh I've been sitting here for close upon two year,
And I wish I were in my coffin underground.
I've tried to learn the lingo but it's fairly got my goat,
The only thing that I can say's " Roll on that *maknoon* boat ! "
I've got those Shaibah Blues, Shaibah Blues,
I'm fed up, and I'm tired out, and I'm old.

———

*Three songlets from the Middle East. The first is sung when someone boasts,
the second when someone lies, the third when someone wants something—
e.g., expresses a desire for beer.*

THREE SONGLETS

Comrades don't believe him,
    Comrades don't believe him,
Comrades don't believe him,
    He's shooting a ruddy good line !

———

Lying basket, lying basket,
    Roll on that ruddy boat !

———

Not entitled, not entitled,
    Roll on that ruddy boat !

———

*A songlet from India, with the inevitable " roll on the boat that takes me
home " theme.*

JUST THREE MORE DAYS TO GO

Just three more days to go,
And they're going bloomin' slow—
    Roll on the SS. Tora *peechi*.
Oh, mosquitoes, bugs and flies
All get in your ruddy eyes—
    Roll on the boat that takes me home

Written by A. C. Kermode, with music by R. H. Cort, for the comic opera "Flat Out," produced at R.A.F. Station, Halton, by aircraft apprentices in April, 1930, and reproduced from "The Halton Song Book."

THE RIGGERS' SONG

Oh! Oh! O - le- o. What do we do, and what do we know?
Jigs, Jigs, sy-rup of figs, giving ourselves a dig in the ribs, The

Stag - ger and In - ci - dence, struts and ties, All
at - mos-phere is clear and bright

trem-ble be-neath our vig - il - ant eyes.
So is our knowledge of The - ory of Flight.

Fu - se - la-ges keep their spines, All a-long their da - tum lines,
Wings which sometimes as you know, Will in-sist on fly - ing low,

While di-he-dral, if you please, sets it - self at three de-grees.
To e-lim-in-ate our doubt, wash themselves both in and out.

CHORUS

Sing with loud tri-um-phant pealings, Let your sluggish wind-pipes go,

Let us vent our Rig-gers feel-ings With a lus-ty O - le - o

All our worries fade be-fore us, Trouble to the winds we throw,

When we sing the Rigger's chorus, O - le - o - le - o - le - o.

Oh! Oh! Oleo.   What do we do, and what do we know?
Stagger and Incidence, struts and ties,
All tremble beneath our vigilant eyes.
Fuselages keep their spines,
All along their datum lines,
While dihedral, if you please,
Sets itself at three degrees.
Jigs, Jigs, syrup of figs,
Giving ourselves a dig in the ribs.
The atmosphere is clear and bright,
So is our knowledge of Theory of Flight.
Wings which sometimes, as you know,
Will insist on flying low,
To eliminate our doubt,
Wash themselves both in and out.

Chorus: Sing with loud triumphant pealings,
Let your sluggish windpipes go.
Let us vent our Riggers' feelings
With a lusty Oleo,
All our worries fade before us,
Trouble to the winds we throw,
When we sing the Riggers' Chorus,
O-le-o-le-o-le-o.

FAR AWAY

wore it for an air - man who was far, · far a - way A

round her leg she wore a pur - ple gar - ter, She

wore it for an air - man who was far, far a - way.

Around her leg she wore a purple garter,
   She wore it in the springtime and in the month of May.
And if you asked her why the hell she wore it,
   She wore it for an airman who is far, far away.

Chorus: Far away, far away, far away, far away,
         She wore it for an airman who is far, far away.

Around the block she pushed a baby carriage,
   She pushed it in the springtime and in the month of May,
And if you asked her why the hell she pushed it,
   She pushed it for an airman who is far, far away.

       Far away, far away, far away, far away,
       She pushed it for an airman who is far, far away.

Behind the door her father kept a shotgun,
   He kept it in the springtime and in the month of May,
And if you asked him why the hell he kept it,
   He kept it for an airman who is far, far away.

       Far away, far away, far away, far away,
       He kept it for an airman who is far, far away.

Upon his grave she placed a bunch of flowers,
  She placed it in the springtime and in the month of May,
And if you asked her why the hell she placed it,
  She placed it for an airman who is *six feet down.*

    Six feet down, six feet down, six feet down, six feet down,
    She placed it for an airman who is six feet down.

———

*Written by A. C. Kermode, with music by R. H. Cort, for the comic opera
"Flat Out," produced at R.A.F. Station, Halton, by aircraft apprentices
in April, 1930, and reproduced here from "The Halton Song Book."*

THE COPPERSMITHS' SONG

CHORUS

Tin, tin, bashers of tin, Tin, tin, du-ra-mu-lin.

Cop-per-smiths and sheet metal workers, We are Halton's toughest workers,

Tin, tin, bashers of tin, Tin, tin, du - ra - mu - lin.

We a - lone are real - ly truth - ful, When we say our trade is use - ful,

Tin, tin, bashers of tin, Tin, tin, du - ra - mu - lin.

Fine

Verses 1 to 5

Bring your surplus scraps of metal, Bring your tongs or old tin kettle.

124

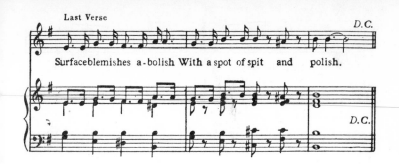

Last Verse

Surface blemishes a-bolish With a spot of spit and polish.

D.C.

Chorus: Tin, Tin, Bashers of Tin,
         Tin, Tin, Duralumin,
         Coppersmiths and sheet metal workers,
         We are Halton's toughest workers,
         Tin, Tin, Bashers of Tin,
         Tin, Tin, Duralumin,
         We alone are really truthful,
         When we say our trade is useful,
         Tin, Tin, Bashers of Tin,
         Tin, Tin, Duralumin.

Verses:

1. Bring your surplus scraps of metal,
   Bring your tongs or old tin kettle.

2. We will guarantee to mend it,
   Bash it, mould it, break it, bend it.

3. In our furnaces we'll heat it,
   Then with hammers we will beat it.

4. Carefully we'll shape or size it,
   Temper it or normalise it.

5. Join it with a skill amazing,
   Welding, soldering or brazing.

6. Surface blemishes abolish,
   With a spot of spit and polish.

Sung by 38 and other squadrons in India and elsewhere in the early 1930's to the tune of " In Jersey City."

A MAIDEN YOUNG AND FAIR

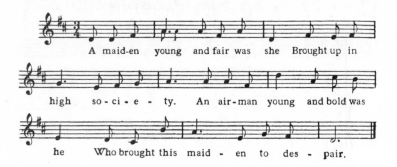

A maid-en young and fair was she Brought up in high so-ci-e-ty. An air-man young and bold was he Who brought this maid-en to des-pair.

A maiden young and fair was she
  Brought up in high society.
An airman young and bold was he
  Who brought this maiden to despair.

Now when her apron strings would meet
  He'd walk with her through snow and sleet ;
But when those strings they would not meet
  He'd pass her by out in the street.

Her father coming home one night
  Did find his house without a light.
He went upstairs to go to bed
  When suddenly he turned his head.

He went into his daughter's room
  And found her hanging by a rope.
He took his knife and cut her down,
  And on her breast he found this note :

" I wish my baby had been born
  Before my troubles had begun.
So dig my grave both wide and deep
  And lay white lilies at my feet."

Now listen, all you airmen bold,
  A true maid's love is hard to find,
So when you find one good and true,
  Don't change the old one for the new.

Written by someone under the pseudonym " Columns," with music by R. H. Cort, for the comic opera " Flat Out," produced at R.A.F. Station, Halton, by aircraft apprentices in April, 1930, and reproduced here from " The Halton Song Book."

A FORCED LANDING

Ailerons are busted, cockpit's round the fin,
Fuselage is twisted, tank's a lot of tin,
Plugs are in the compass, floats inside the sump,
Quite a perfect landing !
Crash ! Smash ! Bump !

Undercarriage broken, mixed up with the mag ;
Centre section's crumpled, plane's a mass of rag,
Prop inside the crankcase, shaft a molten lump,
Oh, a proper landing !
Crash ! Smash ! Bump !

Pilot quite unshaken, doesn't care a hoot,
But a trifle sore with nuts inside his boot :
In our kind of service we don't get the hump
In a simple landing—
Crash ! Smash ! Bump !

------

*Sung by Royal Air Force mechanical transport drivers to the hymn tune
" Oft in Danger, Oft in Woe."*

THE M.T. DRIVERS' SONG

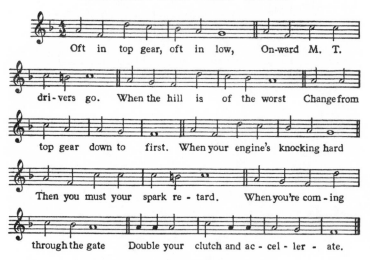

Oft in top gear, oft in low, Onward M. T. drivers go. When the hill is of the worst Change from top gear down to first. When your engine's knocking hard Then you must your spark re-tard. When you're coming through the gate Double your clutch and ac-cel-ler-ate.

Oft in top gear, oft in low,
Onward M.T. drivers go.
When the hill is of the worst,
Change from top gear down to first.
When your engine's knocking hard
Then your spark you must retard.
When you're coming through the gate
Double de-clutch and accelerate.

An airman's mess song from Iraq. When airmen from Home arrived on posting, dirty and unkempt after their travels, they would be kitted in the illest-fitting garb and then, in the canteen, the oldest member of the squadron would sing to them this depressing ditty to the tune of " My Sleepy Valley."

SONG TO NEWCOMERS TO IRAQ

Now, to you who have just arrived,
    Listen to one who has survived :
Don't volunteer for another year in Iraq.
    For they'll put you on the Grim,
Looking pale and ruddy thin,
    And they'll say, " What luck !
    He's as pure as muck—
    He's from Iraq."
There's nothing but *mhutti* and gloom everywhere,
You'll gaze at your tent-pole, all filled with despair—
For they'll put you out on the Grim
    Looking pale and ruddy thin,
    And they'll say, " What luck !
    He's as pure as muck—
    He's from Iraq."

A flying training song of affection for the Avro, to the tune of " That Old-fashioned Mother of Mine."   See a later parody on page 152 .

THAT OLD-FASHIONED AVRO OF MINE

There are fellows who swear at machines in the air,
At mechanics who rig them and don't seem to care.
But there's a machine which is oily and slow,
And it's locked in the heart of a tree that I know.

> Just an old-fashioned Avro with old-fashioned ways,
> And a kick that says, " Back-fire " to you,
> An old Mono engine that konks out and stays
> When the toil of a long flight is through.
> Though the pressure will drop and it loses its prop
> And the pilot's inclined to resign,
> I'll rejoice till I die—that I learnt how to fly
> On that old-fashioned Avro of mine !

There are finer machines with much better wind-screens,
And whose pilots don't know what a dud engine means,
But my good old Avro can loop, roll or spin,
There isn't a field that I can't put it in.

Sung by 43 Squadron to the tune of " Sussex by the Sea " from about 1936.
The squadron was stationed at Tangmere, Sussex, 1925/42 *and* 1949/51.

A SONG OF FORTY-THREE

We'll defend your blue skies
    Over land and sea,
Through shot and shell we'll fight like hell,
    And merry men are we.
So if you go to Sussex,
    Whoever you may be,
You can tell them all that we'll fight or fall
    In the Fighting Forty-Three.

Chorus :
    So here's to the Fighting Forty-Three,
    Up from Sussex by the Sea :
    You can tell them all that we'll fight or fall
    In the Fighting Forty-Three.

Dating from the late 1930's *and widely known in the ranks from that time.*
Tune unknown.

THE AIRMEN'S PRAYER

The first thing we'll pray for
We'll pray for some beer,
Glorious, glorious, glorious beer !
If we only have one beer
May we also have ten,
May we have a blinking brewery !
Said the airmen " Amen."

The next thing we'll pray for
We'll pray for some girls,
Glorious, glorious, glorious girls !
If we only have one girl
May we also have ten,
May we have a blinking harem !
Said the airmen " Amen."

The next thing we'll pray for
We'll pray for the Queen,
The glorious, glorious, glorious Queen !
If she only has one son
May she also have ten,
May she have a blinking squadron !
Said the airmen, " Amen."

The last thing we'll pray for
We'll pray for the erk,
The poor wretched blighter who does all the work.
If he only serves one year
May he also serve ten,
May he serve for blinking ever !
Said the airmen " Amen."

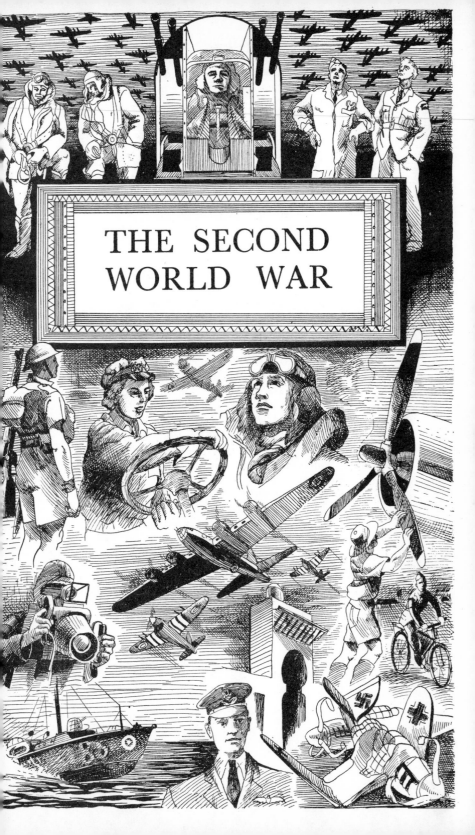

THE SECOND
WORLD WAR

" Bless 'Em All " *was the most widely sung song in the R.A.F. in the second World War, with endless variations in the lyric to suit time, place, squadron, station, etcetera. The song originated in the Royal Naval Air Service in* 1916, *and was the unofficial trooping song long before it was published. Here are two typical versions.*

BLESS 'EM ALL

(Bomber Version)
A Lancaster leaving the Ruhr
Bound for old Blighty shore,
Heavily-laden with *flak*-frightened crew,
Scared stiff and prone on the floor.
There's many a bomber long finished his tour,
There's many a plonk signing on,
We'll get no promotion this side of the ocean,
So cheer up, my lads, Bless 'Em All.

Chorus :   Bless 'Em All, Bless 'Em All,
The long and the short and the tall,
Bless all the Sergeants and W.O. Ones,
Bless all the aircrew and their blinkin' sons,
For we're saying good-bye to them all
As back to our airfields we crawl,
We'll get no promotion this side of the ocean,
So cheer up, my lads, Bless 'Em All.

(Coastal Command Version)
There's many a Hudson just leaving Norway
Bound for old Iceland's shore,
Heavily laden with terrified men
Scared stiff and prone on the floor.
There's many a Heinkel a'pumping out lead,
And many a Messerschmitt too,
They shot off our panties,
And mucked up our scanties,
So cheer up, my lads, Bless 'Em All.

A few Q.D.M.'s and some jolly good luck
Brought us back to old Iceland's shore.
The cloud it was ten-tenths right down on the deck,
And tried very hard to be more.
The ruddy Controllers are driving me mad,
They don't know a map from a chart,
They sit swilling tea, bawling rubbish at me,
They wince at the flight of a dart.
They think that a sextent's a man of the Church,
And a bearing's a little steel ball.
If you talk about bomb-sight
They think that you're half tight
'Cos bombs ain't got no eyes at all.

---

*Written by Corporal J. Holdsworth and sung in a fighter station revue, 1940.
Typical example of a song that dispels gloom by highlighting with humour
and music the airman's grouses.*

IT'S JUST THE AIR FORCE WAY

If you're billeted in barns with pigeons overhead,
    It's Just the Air Force Way.
If the blighters don't drop leaflets but something else instead,
    It's Just the Air Force Way.
If fifty Waafs arrive in camp, as we have heard they might,
And Accommodation want to know where they can spend the night,
And the N.C.O.s take on the job and then put out the light—
    It's Just the Air Force Way.

If you're sent to strike a tent, then put it up again,
    It's Just the Air Force Way.
If a job for one man is given to nine or ten,
    It's Just the Air Force Way.
If you're put on Crash Guard on a night that's dark and damp,
And rushed off in a lorry up to Berwick with a lamp
Then hear the kite has hit the deck a mile outside the camp,
    It's Just the Air Force Way.

If the laundry sends your shirt back looking like a sack,
    It's Just the Air Force Way.
If you send three collars and only get one back,
    It's Just the Air Force Way.
If it rains for days on end and the camp is full of water,
If your boots are covered up with mud, and clay, and mortar,
If airmen cannot get a bath as often as they oughter—
    It's Just the Air Force Way.

If an airman comes along and pinches half your kit,
  It's Just the Air Force Way.
If it takes you weeks and weeks to get a blinkin' chit,
  It's Just the Air Force Way.
If you find the culprit and his quick denial angers,
Don't report the blighter and get him 7 days' jankers,
Just take him on the tarmac and kick him in the hangars—
  It's Just the Air Force Way.

The public's impression is that pilots are always enamoured of their aircraft.
The impression is incorrect, especially if the aircraft is obsolescent, slow or
otherwise " ropey."   This songlet is sometimes chorused, the name of the
aircraft being changed according to circumstances.   Sung to the tune " My
Bonnie."

OLD ANNIE

My An-son's flown ov-er the o-cean,—
— My An-son's lost ov-er the sea,—
— My An-son lies un-der the o-cean,—
— Don't bring back my An-son to me.— Don't
bring back, don't bring back, don't
bring back my An-son to me, to me; Don't
bring back, don't bring back, don't
bring back my An-son to me.—

My Anson's flown over the Ocean,
   My Anson's lost over the Sea,
My Anson lies under the Ocean,
   Don't bring back my Anson to me.

———

A song parody sung in various Home messes from about 1940. *It is one of the few examples of songs sung by aircrew about airwomen, but only in privacy far removed from anyone who may misinterpret it as anything but what it is— a " naughty " song significant of the mood of the singer only and not of the behaviour of those sung about. Done with strong Irish accent. To the tune of " The Mountains of Mourne."*

OH! MARY, THIS WAAF

Oh! Mary, this Waaf is a wonderful life,
   Sure you might get a job as an officer's wife.
There are plenty of airwomen digging for gold,
   At least, when I asked 'em, it's what I was told.
So I soon took a hand in this digging, y'ken,
   And I tried very hard to attract all the men,
I saluted quite smartly by winking one eye,
   But ignored all the airmen unless they could fly.

A young Flight Lieutenant was the cause of my fall,
   So handsome, attractive and heavenly tall,
Took me for a ride in his little M.G.,
   When something went wrong with the engine, y'see.
We were running on Pool and 100 octane,*
   Though I shouted quite loudly no help could obtain.
He'd twenty E.A.s to his credit already,
   So one little Waaf couldn't make him unsteady.

And now on my story I will not enlarge,
   Sufficient to say how I got my discharge.

E.A. =Enemy aircraft.   100 *octane* =aviation spirit.   *Pool* =War-standard motor spirit.

Sung by 285 *and other squadrons from about the time of the Battle of Britain,* 1940, *and derived from two older songs, the American* " *Big Rock Candy Mountains* " *and the English* " *Bells of Hell.*" *Compare with* " *The Last Lay of the Sopwith Camel Pilot,*" 1917-18.

BESIDE AN ESSEX WATERFALL

not com-plete - ly dead,   A   ser - geant pi - lot
sit a - round and sing,   And there - are loads of

closed his   eyes   and this   is   what he   said:
wo – men   too   Oh death where is   thy   sting?

Oh   death where is   thy   sting - a - ling - a - ling,   Oh

grave thy vic - to - ry?   The   bells of   hell   goes

ting - a - ling - a - ling   for   you   but   not   for   me.

Fine

5th VERSE

I asked death if she'd mar-ry me, but all that she would say was ting - a - ling - a - ling, ling, ling, a - ting a - ling all day.

Beside an Essex waterfall one bright September morn
There lay a shattered Hurricane,
Its wings all bent and torn.
And underneath the wreckage, yet not completely dead,
A Sergeant Pilot closed his eyes
And this is what he said :

I'm going to a better place where everything is bright,
Where whisky grows on coconut trees
And you drink beer every night.
Where there is nothing else to do but sit around and sing,
And there are loads of women too—
Oh death where is thy sting ?

Oh Death where is thy sting-a-ling-a-ling,
Oh grave thy victory ?
The bells of hell go ting-a-ling-a-ling
For you but not for me.

I asked Death if she'd marry, marry me,
But all that she would say
Was " Ting-a-ling-a-ling-a-ling
A-ting-a-ling-a-ling " all day.

Written by two aircraftmen—words by Sid Collins and music by Ronnie Aldrich—and later sung in the Eric Maschwitz production " New Faces." Expresses, so sadly, the unsatisfied desire of many ground staff to remuster to aircrew. Published 1940 by the Peter Maurice Music Co.

IF I ONLY HAD WINGS

Ever since the day you're sworn in
Much too early in the morning
Someone wakes you, shiv'ring, yawning, sleepy little heads.
Back upon the pillow falling,
Can you hear a voice a'calling?
It's the Sergeant gently bawling, " Stand beside your beds ! "
Rise and shine, ain't it fine !
You've gotta get up,
You've gotta get out
Before you know what it's all about.
Hurry and dress, the Sergeant's raving,
Over boots and buttons slaving,
No hot water left for shaving—
" Get out on parade ! "
In the kitchen washing dishes,
Peeling spuds and cleaning fishes,
I just keep on making wishes,
Wish I had a trade.
All day long I sing this plaintive song—
I look thro' the window, and look at the sky,
I wish, and I wish, oh, I wish I could fly !

Chorus:
If I only had wings !
Oh, what a diff'rence it would make to things.
All day long I'd be in the sky,
Up on high,
Talking to the birdies that pass me by.
How the fellows would stare
To see me roaring past them thro' the air.
Never tiring of the thrill it brings,
If I only had wings !
I'd be so fearless and bold
That when the stories of my deeds were told
You'd see my picture in the papers,
And they would proudly say,
" The R.A.F. and me just had another good day."
If I only had wings !
One little pair of those elusive things,
You would never hear me complain again—
If I only had wings !
If I only had wings !

Perhaps the classic of Coastal Command—this version from 269 Squadron. There are many variations—note the similarity between it and " A Malta Song," page 184 . Most aircrew songs evidence a " browned-off" attitude towards higher formations (viz., Wing Headquarters) and personnel in Operations Room, Headquarters, etc., but the sentiments expressing this, though usually violent need not be taken too seriously. Sung to the tune of " John Brown's Body."

THE FIRTH OF FLAMING FORTH

We had been fly - ing all day long At a
hun - dred flam - ing feet, __ The wea - ther flam - ing
aw - ful, flam - ing rain and flam - ing
sleet, __ The com - pass it was swing-ing flam - ing
South and flam-ing North, But we made a flam - ing
land fall In the Firth of flam - ing Forth.

CHORUS
Ain't __ the Air Force flam - ing aw - ful?
Ain't __ the Air Force flam - ing aw - ful?

Ain't_ the flam-ing Air Force aw - ful?_ We

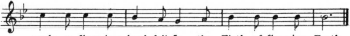

made a flam-ing land fall In the Firth of flam-ing Forth.

We had been flying all day long
   At a hundred flaming feet,
The weather flaming awful,
   Flaming rain and flaming sleet,
The compass it was swinging
   Flaming South and flaming North,
But we made a flaming landfall
   In the Firth of Flaming Forth.
              Ain't the Air Force flaming awful?
              We made a flaming landfall
              In the Firth of Flaming Forth.

We flew the North Atlantic
   Till it made us flaming weep,
The sea was flaming wet,
   And flaming cold and flaming deep.
Operations Room at Thirty Wing
   Is simply flaming rotten,
And Two-Six-Nine will be there
   Till they're flaming well forgotten.
              Ain't the Air Force flaming awful?
              Two-Six-Nine will be there
              Till they're flaming well forgotten.

We joined the flaming Air Force
   'Cos we thought it flaming right,
But we do not care if we fly
   Or if we flaming fight.
But what we do object to
   Are those flaming Ops Room twots
Who sit there sewing stripes on
   At the rate of flaming knots.
              Ain't the Air Force flaming awful?
              They sit there sewing stripes on
              At the rate of flaming knots.

A Coastal Command air/sea rescue song from Iceland, widely sung in messes from 1941, *written by Squadron Leader Charles Bardswell,* 269 *Squadron. The tune of " The Farmer's Boy."*

THE LINDHOLME BUOY

We get the gen from Ops Room when
A Whitley takes the air.
We know for sure from times before
It won't stay long up there.
They are up the creek with a glycol leak,
And the wireless gives no joy.
The A.O.C. says : " Out to Sea
And drop a Lindholme Buoy,
And drop a Lindholme Buoy."

The exactor's duff, the wireless rough,
They're losing height like hell.
The second sprog has used the bog,
The oil begins to smell.
If they hit the drink they are bound to sink,
So it's " 269 Ahoy !"
And out to sea in a Hudson Three
To drop a Lindholme Buoy,
To drop a Lindholme Buoy.

The rum's aboard, the dinghy stored,
So taxi out and go.
The flare path's lit, the weather's fit,
The runways cleared of snow.
One engine's gone, they're limping on
Across the Flaxa Flow.
So we'll miss our tea and out to sea
To drop a Lindholme Buoy,
To drop a Lindholme Buoy.

The Ops Room phone's no need for moans,
They're down at Reykjavik,
The rescue crew say : " Good thing too
We thought we'd miss the Flicks."
And who can say perhaps one day
That Whitley they'll employ
To fly to sea and rescue me
And drop a Lindholme Buoy,
And drop a Lindholme Buoy.

The rescue crew are in a stew,
The rocket's in the sky,
The voices boom in the old Ops Room,
And we are asking why.
You can hear them say " It's off for today "
So you won't have to fly,
The Whitley's home on Reyki's 'drome
Without a Lindholme Buoy,
Without a Lindholme Buoy.

———

Another Women's Auxiliary Air Force reception centre song, to the tune of
" *John Peel.*"

IN THE WOMEN'S AUXILIARY AIR FORCE

There is a Service, brave and true
Which shows us what the girls can do,
They're got us now and they've got you too—
In the Women's Auxiliary Air Force.

We love our corporals, we love Flight Sarge,
We love our sausages and we love our marge,
We love our beds so soft and large—
In the Women's Auxiliary Air Force.

We march along the Prom all day,
And though " Eyes Front " the corporals say,
We've seen the whole of Morecambe Bay—
In the Women's Auxiliary Air Force.

Our hair we fasten in a net,
Our shoes and buttons we ne'er forget,
Our turn-out's really smart, you bet—
In the Women's Auxiliary Air Force.

Pay day always brings a smile,
But from innoc. we'd run a mile,
F.F.I.* is such a trial—
In the Women's Auxiliary Air Force.

We've lost our glamour and we've lost our curls,
We can't wear civvies and we can't wear pearls,
They've made us into real tough girls—
In the Women's Auxiliary Air Force.

* F.F.I. – Free from infection

KISS THE BOYS GOOD-BYE

Corporal may I stay out late ?
  It's getting near our posting date,
Please let a poor Waaf celebrate,
   To kiss the RAF goodbye.

Corporal must I cut my hair ?
  Carry ground sheet and my greatcoat wear ?
Let the poor Waaf be without a care
   To kiss the RAF goodbye.

Now I want you to understand me,
From a liberal point of view,
For I'm breaking it to them gently
That we get our style from you.
Corporal, please remember this :
All your rookies you are going to miss,
And kiss you all goodbye.

We volunteered, we volunteered,
We volunteered to join the Air Force.
Ten bob a week, not enough to eat,
Big black shoes and blisters on our feet.
We volunteered, we volunteered,
We volunteered to join the Air Force.
If it wasn't for the war
We'd be where we were before—
Waafie—you're barmy !

There are many versions of " Ops in a Wimpey " or " Ops in a Whitley."
This is one, from 156 Squadron. The Compiler especially likes the fourth verse,
the last line of the sixth verse, and the hope expressed in the last verse that bad
weather will permit the proposed operation to be cancelled. Sung to the tune
of " Waltzing Matilda."

OPS IN A WIMPEY

Who'll fly a Wimpey, who'll fly a Wimpey,
   Who'll fly a Wimpey over Germany?
I, said the Pilot, I, said the Pilot,
   I'll fly a Hercules Mark Three.

Chorus: Who'll come a doing-ing, who'll come a doing-ing,
         Who'll come a doing-ing, a doing-ing with me?
         I'll come a doing-ing, I'll come a doing-ing,
         I'll come a doing-ing in our Mark Three.

I'll pump the oil, Sir, I'll pump the oil, Sir,
I'll pump the oil, said the first W/op to me,
I'll take the rations out to the kite, Sir,
I'll get the rations from our Padree.

I'll set the course, Sir, I'll set the course, Sir,
I'll set the course on my little C.S.C.
If you fly in on the course I set, Sir,
That will take us o'er *flak-ee.*

I'll shoot 'em down, Sir, I'll shoot 'em down, Sir,
I'll shoot 'em down if they don't shoot at me :
Then we'll go to Ops room and shoot a horrid line, Sir,
And then we'll all get the D.F.C.

I'll press the *tit*, Sir, I'll press the *tit*, Sir,
I'll press the *tit* at the first *flak* we see,
'Cos I don't like *flak*, Sir, I don't like *flak*, Sir,
Nothing but bags of height for me.

Let's do our air test, let's do our air test,
Let's go on up and do our N.F.T.
Then we'll go to Holkham and shoot off fifty rounds, Sir,
(And save a few for H.Q. Group 3).

What about the Met, Sir, what about the Met, Sir,
What about the Met, it seems dud to me ?
Let's scrub it out, Sir, let's scrub it out, Sir,
'Cos I've got date with my popsee.

Like the preceding song, sung to the tune of " Waltzing Matilda " by 51, 77, 102 and other Squadrons. The last two lines of each chorus repeat the last two lines of the preceding verse.

OPS IN A WHITLEY

Boldly

The first sil - ly blight - er got in - to his ae - ro -plane,

Said he would fly_____ ov - er Ger - ma -ny, And he

sang as he swang and pranged it on the boun - da - ry,

"Who'll come on ops in a Whit - ley with me?"

CHORUS

Ops in a Whit - ley, ops in a Whit - ley,

Spoken Prologue : Once upon a time there were six Keen Operational Types, all intent on Flying a Dangerous Mission, not to mention Dicing with Death.   Now—

The first silly blighter got into his aeroplane,
Said he would fly over Germany,
And he sang as he swang and pranged it on the boundary,
" Who'll come on Ops in a Whitley with me ?"

Chorus :   Ops in a Whitley, Ops in a Whitley,
      Who'll come on Ops in a Whitley with me ?
      And he sang as he swang and pranged it on the boundary,
      " Who'll come on Ops in a Whitley with me ?"

The second silly blighter got into the air all right,
Flew over Flamborough and crashed it in the sea,
And they sang as they swam right up and down the coast and back,
" Who'll come on Ops in a Whitley with me ?"

Chorus (with the last two lines of verse as above)

151

The third silly blighter got out over Germany,
Up came the *flak* like a Christmas tree,
And the Wireless Op. cried as the Captain quite forgot himself,
" Who'll come on Ops in a Whitley with me ?"

Chorus (with last two lines of verse as above)

The fourth silly blighter flew out over Hanover,
Up came the fighters, one, two, three,
And the Rear Gunner cried as he buckled on his parachute,
" Who'll come on Ops in a Whitley with me ?"

Chorus (with last two lines of verse as above)

The fifth silly blighter he got over Magdeburg,
They couldn't find the target and dropped 'em in the sea,
And the Navigator cried as the Captain tried to shoot himself,
" Who'll come on Ops in a Whitley with me ?"

Chorus

The sixth silly blighter he got there and back all right,
They gave him a Green but he couldn't see the " T,"
And he sang midst the flames as he pranged it on the hangar-roof,
" Who'll come on Ops in a Whitley with me ?"

Chorus

———

A pretty little bomber parody sung by 70 *Squadron in* 1941 *in the Middle East to the tune of " That Old Fashioned Mother of Mine." See also a predecessor, " Old-Fashioned Bristol," India,* 1919, 28 *Squadron.*

OLD FASHIONED WIMPEY

There's an old-fashioned Wimpey
   With old-fashioned wings,
With a fuselage tattered and torn.
   She's got old-fashioned engines
All tied up with strings,
   It's a wonder she was ever air-borne.
Still, she's quite safe and sound
   'Cos she won't leave the ground,
And there's something that makes her divine :
   For the Huns up above were all taught how to love
That old-fashioned Wimpey of mine.

Written and sung by WAAF officers on a Gas Course, 1941, to the tune of the same.

THANKS FOR THE MEMORY

Thanks for the memory
Of journeys made in hate, up to the Gas School gate,
Of many tears, and many fears, of what would be our fate
E-ternal Memory.
Of respirator drill, which shook but did not kill,
Of perfumes that weren't lethal.   But, O Lord
They made us ill.
Pathetic it was.

Then we began to take interest,
The instructors have got what it takes !
We suddenly knew they were human,
We thought them Hell but found them Swell !
So thanks for the memory,
And strictly *entre nous*, they'll do as much for you—
We'd never have believed it, but we're sorry that it's through
So thank you so much.

Night-fighter song from early in the war.   Probably originated with 141
(Beaufighter) Squadron.   Sung by 43 *and other Squadrons up to* 1947,
*especially when there were night-fighter pilots about.   To the tune of " So
Early in the Morning."*

ORBITTING THE BEACON

Num - ber one had got a Beau★ Fit - ted with a
gun or so. Will it fire?___ Oh dear no, So he's
CHORUS
or - bit - ting the bea - con. Or - bit - ting the bea - con,
Or - bit - ting the bea - con, It's quite all - right in the
mid - dle of the night, Or - bit - ting the bea - con.

*Beau = Beaufighter aircraft

Number One had got a Beau
Fitted with a gun or so.
Will it fire ?   Oh dear no,
So he's orbitting the beacon.

Chorus :   Orbitting the beacon,
Orbitting the beacon,
It's quite all right in the middle of the night,
Orbitting the beacon.

Number Two had a flying start,
A ditch wiped off his undercart,
Now all night with a quaking heart,
He's orbitting the beacon.

Chorus

Number Three has got a blip,
A Maggie on a training trip,
But it's given him the slip,
So he's orbitting the beacon.

Chorus

———

Sung by plotters in the operations room of 616 *Squadron,* 1941, *to the tune of* " *Lover Come Back to Me.*"

HEINKEL COME BACK TO ME

The sky was blue and way up high
A Heinkel flew up in the sky,
And in the Ops Room they were saying :
  " Heinkel where can you be ?"

It came at last o'er Kirton's 'drome,
It flew right past on its way home,
And, way back, Hitler he was saying :
  " Heinkel come back to me."

When dear Joner on the tannoy told us of this plane
Station Defence was so delighted.
Shippers sent up all his Spitfires and a Hurricane
Who said : " One enemy is sighted."

The clouds were low, the sky was grey,
That ruddy plane, it got away,
But in the sea it fell—and left Hitler vainly yelling :
  " Heinkel come back to me."

FRAGMENT OF ADVICE

Don't fly at night either fast or slow,
With your boost too high or your revs too low,
Or you'll run out of juice
With a long way to go,
And you'll never get back in the morning.

———

A typical Coastal squadron song. 220 *Squadron sang it in* 1940-41 *when they were operating over the North Sea. The reference in the second verse to* 70 *miles north was (like so many points made in squadron songs) based on fact, the error occurring owing to compass trouble. Sung to the tune of "John Brown's Body."*

A HUDSON SONG

Our___ Flight Com-man - der got the D. F.
C.___ For find - ing a U - Boat in the
I rish sea.___ In - stead of bomb-ing the
bind - er, he went out on the spree, But we
still come roll - ing home.___

CHORUS

Why?__ We're Two__ Twen - ty Squad - ron,

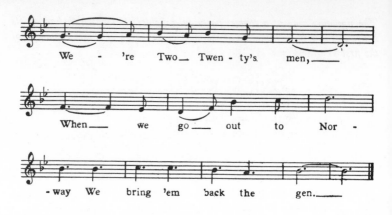

We - 're Two— Twen - ty's. men,—

When— we go — out to Nor -

- way We bring 'em back the gen.—

Our Flight Commander got the D.F.C.
For finding a U-boat in the Irish sea.
Instead of bombing the binder he went out on the spree,
But we still come rolling home.

Chorus: Why?   We're Two-Twenty Squadron,
We're Two-Twenty's men,
When we go out to Norway
We bring 'em back the gen.

Our navigators have no goddam ruddy worth,
They make their blinkin' landfalls always 70 miles north,
Instead of landing at their base they hit the Firth of Forth,
But we still come rolling home.

Our wireless operators never panic when
The captain shouts, " Oi, quick, me boys, a Q.D.M.,"
They know they're lost but, dammit chaps, they also know their gen,
And we still come rolling home.

Our rear gunners think it's lots of blinkin' fun
Sitting in the turret waiting for the Blinkin' Hun,
Until the binder comes along and they miss the son of a gun,
But we still come rolling home.

The signature song of a concert party on a fighter station which had as its badge a Tiger in perpetuation of the memory of the 74 or Tiger Squadron of the first World War.

ONE FOR THE TIGER

One for the Tiger, so Hip-hip-hooray !
One for the Tiger to finish the day !
When we say three cheers we really mean four,
We always have enough breath to squeeze in one more.
Think of the Tiger when things appear black—
He always goes forward, He never goes back—
Forward to happiness, Into the Fray—
One for the Tiger !
Hip-hip-hooray !

This superb parody originated at R.A.F. Station, Habbaniyah, Iraq, in 1940, and afterwards was adopted and adapted by stations throughout the Middle East. The service was conducted with great solemnity. It was dictated to the compiler by rote by a Squadron Leader who had officiated on so many occasions that he knew the whole thing off by heart.

SERVICE OF THANKSGIVING FOR SAFE ARRIVAL IN IRAQ

Order of Service.

1. Organ Voluntary : *The Dead March in Saul.*

2. *Chaplain:* We will commence our service by singing hymn No. 252 to the tune of " There is a green hill far away."

> There are some greenhorns far away
> All sitting in a Boat,
> Just like the one that brought us here—
> So let's sit back and gloat.—AIRMEN.

3. *Chaplain:* Dearly beloved brethren, I humbly pray and beseech you as many as are here present to accompany me with a glorious thirst and some ready cash unto the bar of the Service Institute, saying after me :

> " Almighty and most merciful Records, we have heard and obeyed thy commands like lost sheep ; we have followed too much the vices and desires of our own hearts, and there is no wealth in us. We have done those things we ought not to have done, and left undone those things we ought not to have left undone, and there is no hope in us. But then, O Records,

have mercy upon us, miserable first offenders, restore thou them that are penniless according to thy promises declared unto us in King's Regulations and Air Council Instructions. And grant, O most merciful Records, that we may hereafter lead a goodly, riotous and inebriate life to the glory of thy most perfect filing system."—AIRMEN.

4. *Chaplain:* Let us pray for our reliefs.

Congregation: Hear, hear.

Chaplain: O Captain of the *Somersetshire*, we pray thee to drop not thine anchor in the Shatt-el-Arab, nor to tarry overlong at Kasfret but to make all speed to relieve us from this torment which is ours. We pray thee to attend unceasingly to thy cargo of souls that they may keep and maintain perfect health in body and in mind and not be isolated. This we ask not for their sake but for ours.—AIRMEN.

5. *Chaplain:* Let us pray for the Troopship.

" Almighty Somersetshire, queen of all troopships, we pray thee to spring no leak, neither to capsize, but to preserve thy good servants the Captain, the Crew, the Bo'sun, the Erks and All Other Persons Committed to Thy Charge. And more especially the Sweepers and the Swabbers that they may faithfully discharge their duties to the Bibby Line and our immediate release."—AIRMEN.

6. *Chaplain:* Bear up, for the boat is at hand.

Congregation: O boat roll on to save us.

Chaplain: O boat make speed to take us.

Congregation: And our mouths shall spew forth thy praise.

Chaplain: O Records make haste to post us.

Congregation: As all our trust is in thee.

Chaplain: Glory be to the Captain, the Crew and the Erks.

Congregation: As it was when we came, is now, and is ever likely to be. Will our tour never end?—AIRMEN.

7. *Chaplain:* We will now sing Hymn No. 664B.

O Boat, our curse in ages past,
    Our hope for years to come,
May we recline beneath thy mast,
    And bear us to our home.

These three long years within our sight
    Are like a lifetime gone,
Long as the guards we did at night,
    So Boat do please roll on.

O Boat, our curse in ages past,
Our hope for years to come,
Let's hope the next will be our last,
And leave us safe at home.
—AIRMEN.

8. *Chaplain:* The New Testament lesson commenceth at the fifth verse of the thirteenth chapter of the Air Force Act:

" Now it came to pass in the ancient city of Habbaniyeh that there was a certain poor man who had but little *feluce*. Now at this time the feast of the Goofa was nigh, and the multitude had assembled in the canteen to rejoice. And the poor man was sore depressed because he could not go and do likewise.

" So he did count up his entire wealth and when he had counted it he found he had got but one akker. So he stood himself in the gateway of the canteen and entreated passers-by that they would give him *baksheesh*. But they would not, for they were *moskeen*.

" And it came to pass that a certain rich man, a Fitter One by profession, passed that way, and the poor man said unto him: Lend me, I pray thee, the sum of two akkers for I am athirst.

" But the rich man said : Nay, but I will spin thee for it.

" So the poor man did spin him, and all his disciples were with him and he did win.

" Therefore, I say unto you, Lay not up for yourselves treasures in National Savings Certificates and War Bonds, but rather rejoice whilst ye may."

Here endeth the lesson.

9. *Chaplain:* I will now read the Church Notices :

There will be no Church Services next Sunday as there is a race meeting in Baghdad. My selections are given in the Parish Magazine now on sale at the porch.

The collection today is on behalf of the Warrant Officers' Poor Children's Beer Fund, and you are asked to give generously.

Aircraftwoman Mary Jones is being baptised at the evening service, and the gallery will be closed to onlookers. Members of the congregation are requested to refrain from singing " O Salome " during the ceremony.

10. *Chaplain :* We will now sing Hymn No. 765C.

O Air Ministry strong to save,
Whose airmen sail the restless wave,
We hope the mighty ocean deep
It's own appointed place will keep.
O hear us when we cry to thee
For our reliefs upon the sea.

You Three who have it in your power
Guard our fellows in their dark hour
From rock and tempest, tor-pedo,
Protect them whereso'er they go.
Then evermore we'll cry to thee
When we are also on the sea.

—AIRMEN.

11. *Chaplain :* The text of my sermon this morning is taken from the fifth line of the second paragraph of the thirteenth chapter of the nineteenth section of Station Standing Orders—" He will immediately endeavour to extinguish it."

I wonder how many of you realise what our beloved Commander meant when he wrote these beautiful words of wisdom. Let us analyse the message so that we may gain its full significance : " He will "—any Waaf knows what that may mean ; " immediately "—well, those of you who have been in Iraq know that that just means any time within the next three or four days ; " endeavour "—that means to try ; all our C.O. asks of us is to try ; " extinguish "—that means to put out ; and " it " may mean anything from sex-appeal to the cat, but I think that what was at the back of our beloved Commander's mind was a fire.

So that, on seeing a fire, we are to try within three or four days to put it out.

Now, to put out a fire you require water. I do not know what water is, but it's good for putting out fires and for cooking with. So that, on coming to a new station, you must see that there is an adequate water supply. I remember in the old days, before the irrigation system got cracking, that there was no water on the camp for putting out fires. So our beloved Commander sent us into a far country to purchase a well. After many days of toil and travel we came to a country where there were wells and we bought one and brought it back to the camp. When we arrived we found that they had forgotten to dig a hole for it and there was our beautiful well sticking straight up in the air. When our beloved Commander saw it he waxed wrath and said : " You sink wells." So we dug a deep, deep hole and into the hole we put the well and the well sank to the bottom of the hole and the sand came and covered it up and there was no more well. Our beloved Commander, when he saw what had happened, was sore displeased and he cried out that we had extinguished the wrong blasted thing and posted us. (*Loud cheers.*)

Before trying to put out a fire you must first of all sign for it. This elementary principle of Air Force procedure cannot be too strongly stressed, and to show the importance of it I will tell you a story of the Battle of Hastings.

Harold on his Horse with his Hawk was at Hastings when he discovered that the Air Force had not arrived although they had all been posted home from the Crimea. So he sent to Uxbridge a Most Secret, Most Immediate, To-be-read-in-a-Green-Light-Only signal, instructing the Air Force to Proceed immediately to Hastings. When the signal arrived the Warrant Officer Disciplinary, as usual, was the only person on duty. So he took the signal, signed for it, and took it down to the local pub to have it deciphered, for in those days you required a cash register and a dart board to decode signals. When he found what the message meant he took it back to the camp, woke up the C.O., and in the language of those times asked him " Where the hell is Hastings? " The C.O. said, " At the seaside, and you're in charge of everything," and passed out again. So the Warrant Officer gathered all the erks together and took them to the canteen to rejoice.

In the morning all he could remember was that they had to go to the seaside, and to him that meant one place—Southend. So they threaded and throgged their way through the ancient City of London to Liverpool Street and, as Dirty Dick's wasn't open, they caught the first train to Southend. When they arrived, the erks asked the Warrant Officer what they should do and he said, " Yer dumps yer kits, eats whelks and looks at the sea—that's what yer do at Southend." So the Air Force sat on the front eating whelks and gazing into the far, far distance at the sea.

After many weeks Harold on his Horse with his Hawk arrived at Southend. He was in high dudgeon when he saw the Air Force there. And in his anger he shouted at the Warrant Officer, " I have lost the Battle of Hastings—why weren't you there? " And the Warrant Officer, looking at him as though he were another whelk, replied, " Because I hadn't signed for the bloody thing."

Here endeth the sermon.

12. *Chaplain:* We will now sing Hymn No. 64.

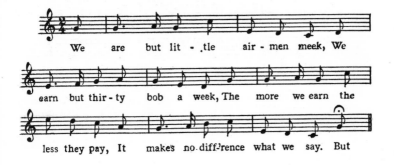

We are but lit - tle air - men meek, We earn but thir - ty bob a week, The more we earn the less they pay, It makes no diff'rence what we say. But

Lord Trenchard loves us, Lord Trenchard loves us,

Lord Trenchard loves us, and so he bloomin' well ought

We are but little airmen meek,
We earn but thirty bob a week,
The more we earn the less they pay—
It makes no difference what we say.
But—Lord Trenchard loves us,
    Lord Trenchard loves us,
    Lord Trenchard loves us,
      And so he bloomin' well ought!

—AIRMEN.

13. *Chaplain:* I will now pronounce the Rigger Mortis. *Salaam Aleekum.*

Congregation: Wa aleekum a Salaam.

Together: Whacko.

———

Typical of overseas squadron songs—with movement from one station to another and longing for the Boat Home the main themes. It originated in the Middle East about 1940.

ON THE MOVE

Pack the e - quip-ment all rea-dy for ship-ment,

We're on the move a-gain.___ For - get your de -
-jec-tion and do an in - spec-tion on ev - er - y
ae - ro - plane.___ Blighty one in the air.___

Pack the equipment all ready for shipment,
We're on the move again ;
Forget your dejection and do an inspection
On every aeroplane.

I wonder where we're moving to,
We don't know.   Who does?   Do you?
However, we'll know when we get there,
And rumours of Blighty are in the air.

We used to be in India
Till we went to Singapore,
Then we moved across to Aden
When the Eyeties joined the war.

Later we went to Egypt,
And after that to Greece,
But, roll on, that Boat for Blighty,
And a spot of bloomin' peace.

Sung particularly by 10, 51 *and* 77 *Squadrons. Written in September,* 1941, *when Whitleys were briefed for daylight bombing. At the time a Whitley had in fact crash-landed on the beach and hit a mine. It is quite impossible to pull a Whitley out of a power dive at* 195, *of course. Whitley* 10*'s are mythical. Sung to the tune of "It's Foolish But It's Fun."*

I LOVE TO FLY A WHITLEY THREE

I love to fly a Whitley Three
In daylight over Germany.
I'd have the M.E.s after me—
It's foolish but it's fun.

There's bags of M.E. One-One-O's
And M.E. One-O-Nine's,
And if you crash-land on the beach
There's always bags of mines.

I love to fly a Whitley Five
And put her in a power dive,
And pull her out at One Nine Five,
It's foolish but it's fun.

I love to fly a Whitley Ten,
I dunno where, I dunno when,
And bomb old Hitler in his den—
It's foolish but it's fun.

Expressing the same sentiment as "If I Only Had Wings," this song was written in 1940 *by the compiler of the present volume for his station concert party.*

THE ERK'S LAMENT

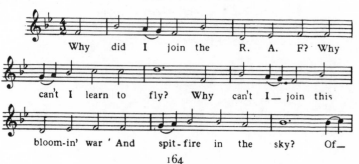

Why did I join the R. A. F? Why can't I learn to fly? Why can't I — join this bloom-in' war ' And spit-fire in the sky? Of —

164

fly - ing **we** do nil all_ day, Our du - ty's on the

ground **Where** ev - en_ Squad-ron - Lead - ers are

ter - ra fir - ma bound.

> Why did I join the R.A.F.?
> Why can't I learn to fly?
> Why can't I join this bloomin' war
> And Spitfire in the sky?
> Of flying we do nil all day,
> Our duty's on the ground
> Where even squadron leaders
> Are terra firma bound.
>
> Of stunting, jinking, we see none,
> Of trips there's even less,
> We spend our time in carting swill
> And sweeping out the mess.
> We're fitters, drivers, Woms and Wops,
> Mechanics and G.D.'s—
> We fill in forms and documents
> And lubricate and grease.
>
> The Warrant Officer is tough,
> And Chiefy's even worse,
> The Corporal carries all the cans,
> The Police are one long curse.
> Why did we join the R.A.F.?
> Why can't we sweep the sky?
> We're browned-off doing ground staff jobs—
> Why can't we learn to fly?

---

*A pretty little concert party type song about a Waaf, written by Flight
Lieutenant John Barnes, and published* 1941 *by the Peter Maurice Music
Company.*

MY A.C.W. 2

It happened one day we were talking,
And before very long we were walking,
'Tho I didn't know where we were walking to,
And I didn't know whom I was talking to.
It was one of those things that just happened that way,
Now the story of our love is like a play.

Chorus: She was full of melody and laughter,
        Dreams were gay and skies were always blue,
        Till other airmen started running after
        My A.C.W.2.
        What a thrilling girl to be in love with,
        But alas, my heart already knew
        That I was not the only one in love with
        My A.C.W.2.
        She assured me there was no other—
        Why should she make believe,
        Then one day she said, " I'm off to see my mother
        On a forty-eight hour leave."
        Then I met a fellow and we tarried,
        He said, " Love is grand when love is new."
        And I discovered why, for he's just married—
        My A.C.W.2.

Sung by the Waaf plotters in the operations room at an R.A.F. station before the enemy blitz on nearby Liverpool in 1941. *It is the duty of these airwomen to plot on large maps the positions of friendly and enemy aircraft as operations proceed. When slack, they knit. Sung to the tune of " The Woodpecker's Song."*

THE PLOTTERS' LAMENT

We're up each morning bright and early,
    We've got to be on watch by eight,
The Controller is so bloomin' surly
    If we are but one moment late.
Chorus: See us hoping for a blitz,
        Hope, hope, hoping for a darn good blitz,
        Otherwise we sits and knits
        All day long.

The airmen say we are not needed,
    They say we're useless as can be,
But there's one thing that should be heeded,
    That's the way we *knit* for Victory.

Sung at Home on isolated R.A.F. stations and units out in the blue from 1940 *onwards. On one station it was sung on the stage by the concert party, a few local civilians were in the audience, they took it quite seriously, and there ensued a local controversy about it for weeks afterwards! Few Service songs are sung seriously, and least of all this one. The place-name in the chorus line is, of course, altered to suit the station's location. The song is, I believe, a parody of an old one called "The Bloody Stockman." To the tune of "Baa, Baa Black Sheep."*

BLOODY HELL

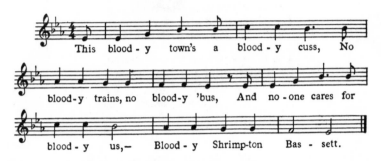

This blood-y town's a blood-y cuss, No blood-y trains, no blood-y 'bus, And no-one cares for blood-y us,— Blood-y Shrimp-ton Bas-sett.

This bloody town's a bloody cuss,
No bloody trains, no bloody bus,
And no one cares for bloody us—
  Bloody Shrimpton-Bassett.

The bloody roads are bloody bad,
The bloody folk are bloody mad,
They'd make the brightest bloody sad—
  Bloody Shrimpton-Bassett.

All bloody clouds, and bloody rains,
No bloody curbs, no bloody drains,
The Council's got no bloody brains—
  Bloody Shrimpton-Bassett.

Eveything's so bloody dear,
A bloody bob for bloody beer,
And is it good? No bloody fear!—
  Bloody Shrimpton-Bassett.

The bloody films are bloody old,
The bloody seats are bloody cold,
You can't get in for bloody gold!—
  Bloody Shrimpton-Bassett.

No bloody sport, no bloody games,
No bloody fun ; the bloody dames
Won't even give their bloody names!—
  Bloody Shrimpton-Bassett.

The bloody dances make you smile,
The bloody band is bloody vile,
It only cramps your bloody style—
  Bloody Shrimpton-Bassett.

Best bloody place is bloody bed
With bloody ice on bloody head,
You might as well be bloody dead !—
  Bloody Shrimpton-Bassett.

The bloody baths are bloody cold,
The bloody news is bloody old,
To tell the truth is bloody bold—
  Bloody Shrimpton-Bassett.

The bloody pub's a bloody scream,
Its comfort's just a bloody dream.
It's bloody—that's just what I mean !—
  Bloody Shrimpton-Bassett.

———

A song of 1941 *when airmen on stations throughout the country were—like everyone else—on defence training, sometimes with improvised arms, against the possibility of Invasion.*   *Written by Corporal J. Holdsworth for a fighter station concert party.*

PRACTICE-FLAPPING

Chorus:
I'm off to the invasion, just show me that invasion,
 And I'll help to keep those blasted Huns at bay.
On this auspish occasion I don't need no persuasion,
 For I've practised Practice-Flapping every day.

I've flapped instead of flipping,
Parades I never shirk,
I've even practised sloping arms when I should be at work,
And if I keep on shooting straight they might make me a clerk !
Now I've practised Practice-Flapping every day.

I've got a secret weapon,
This dangerous screw-picket,
And every time I see a Hun I'll score a middle wicket,
And as I bowl him out he'll say, " Mein Gott ! this isn't cricket !"
Now I've practised Practice-Flapping every day.
And maybe in his fury
The Fuehrer's latest wish
Will be a gas attack on us without our Group's permish ;
So we shall then retaliate by using cookhouse fish !
Now I've practised Practice-Flapping every day.

In most of the out-of-the-way parts of the world in which the Royal Air Force has served, the ubiquitous petrol tin is the solution to most domestic equipment problems. This song—from the Coastal Command squadrons stationed in Iceland from 1941 onwards—bears witness to the variety of uses to which it was put. Written by Flight Lieutenant Pascoe Thornton for a guest night at Kaldardarnes. Sung to the hymn tune " The Church's One Foundation."

THE NISSEN HUT'S FOUNDATION

The Nissen hut's foundation
    Is petrol tins galore,
They are the one salvation
    Of troops on Iceland's shore.
One tin to shave your face in,
    One tin to brew your tea,
One tin is your wash basin,
    One tin your lavatory.

One tin to mark the miles with
    Along that ropey road,
And tins to put your files in
    In cypher or in code,
One tin is for a shelter
    To guard you in a raid,
And at the Mentaskollin
    Ten tins to store your braid.

One tin to warm your feet in,
 And one to shade the light,
One tin to put your seat in,
 And one to house a Flight,
And lastly there is one tin
 We'd like (there'd be none better)
Packed full of lovely popsies
 From the Windmill Theatre.

Gremlins are fabled sprites who plague air crews and ground staff alike.
They were christened by an airman overseas years ago (so the tale has it);
he was opening a bottle of Fremlin's Ale, when the cork and contents lept out,
taking him unawares. He spoonerised as he said, " A gremlin has jumped
out of my Foblin's." This song is from a photographic reconnaissance
unit, 1942.

SONG OF THE GREMLINS

When you're seven miles up in the heavens
 And that's a hell of a lonely spot,
And it's 50 degrees below zero,
 Which isn't exactly hot,
When you're frozen blue like your Spitfire,
 And you're scared a Mosquito pink,
When you're thousands of miles from nowhere,
 And there's nothing below but the drink—
It's then you will see the gremlins,
 Green and gamboge and gold,
Male and female and neuter,
 Gremlins both young and old.

White ones'll wiggle your wing-tips,
 Male ones'll muddle your maps,
Green ones'll guzzle your glycol,
 Females will flutter your flaps,
Pink ones will perch on your perspex,
 And dance pirouettes on your prop.
There's one spherical middle-aged gremlin
 Who spins on your stick like a top.
They'll freeze up your camera shutters,
 They'll bite through your aileron wires,
They'll cause your whole tail to flutter,
 They'll insert toasting forks in your tyres.

This is the song of the gremlins
 As sung by the P.R.U.
Pretty ruddy unlikely to many,
 But fact none the less to the few.

Another Fortress song from a Coastal squadron. It boasts of what the squadron's Fortresses did to the U-boats and that they were not high altitude but long-distance, low-level convoy escorts. It makes a grand chorus to the tune of " Anchors A-weigh."

A FORTRESS SONG

The Fortress will fly again, over the sea,
Flown by our famous squadron—we're on guard at every entry,
We're always on patrol, seeking the Hun,
We'll see they do not get us when they come out of the sun.
Through sun and storm and rain, ice, snow and hail,
We'll always do our job, we never falter, never shirk or fail.

U-boats all keep away, swiftly they flee,
Convoys in safety sail, they know the Fortress is their sentry.
Our kites will prove their worth, down in the drink,
We'll make the Germans rue it ; bomber boys could never do it ;
No thirty thou. for us, no vapour trail,
No Hun can get below, we never leave the room beneath the tail.

Written and sung by officers on an R.A.F. Gas Course, Christmas, 1941,
to the tune of " The Quartermaster's Stores."

GAS, GAS, GAS

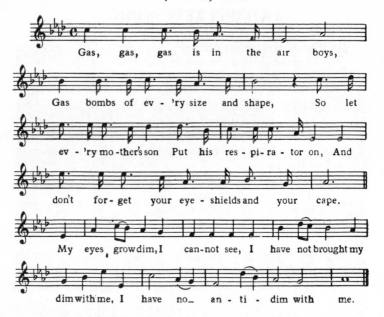

Gas, gas, gas is in the air boys,
    Gas bombs of every size and shape,
So let every mother's son
    Put his respirator on
And don't forget your eyeshields and your cape.

> My eyes grow dim, I cannot see,
> I have not brought my anti-dim with me,
> I have no anti-dim with me.

Rub, rub, rub on Number Two, boys,
    Don't forget to irrigate your eyes,
And if you've work to do
    You can go and see it through,
You're safe from any trouble from the skies.

> My eyes grow bright I now can see,
> You wonder how this comes to be?
> I've found my anti-dim on me.

> So now you see, with all due care,
> I've naught to fear from ground or air,
> I've naught to fear from ground or air.

This is a version of what the Compiler was earnestly assured was the original Flying Fortress Song—there are others. The aircraft concerned was engaged on general reconnaissance and not high level bombing. Sung to the tune of " Lulu."

THE FORTRESS SONG

The Navigator sits in front
    Surrounded by charts true,
Using the larynx microphone
    To blow sweet music through.
Chorus: Prang the ruddy Fortress,
        Prang it good and strong,
        We have to prang the Fortress
        Now the Hudsons are all gone.

The Captain sits on the left side
    Flying the kite at ease,
The Second only gets a chance
    When the Captain gets stiff knees.

The Gunner in mid-upper
    Must stand up whilst he's there,
He only sits when he sits and grits
    His ruddy teeth with fear.

We've also got a Bomb-bay
    With tank and D.C.s too,
And a little rubber hose-pipe
    To bung the gravy through.

The Wireless Op's compartment
    Is warm and snug 'tis said,
And when he gets cheesed off up here
    He's putting in a bed.

The Gunner in the ballock
    Has not got very much room,
But the Doctor says he's better off
    Than he'll be in his tomb.

We've a Gunner in the tail,
    Where room is very sparse,
And every time the wheel retracts
    He moves to let it pass.

Now, there's only one thing needful
And that one thing, you see,
A tube let out of the fuselage,
To jettison the tea.
  Prang the ruddy Fortress,
  Prang it good and strong,
  We have to prang the Fortress
  Now the Hudsons are all gone.

There are many parodies to this tune that incorporate the last two lines. This one, a libel of the Air-Sea Rescue Service of R.A.F., whose magnificent work is famous, should be taken with a pinch of salt. (Sung to the hymn tune " The Church's One Foundation ").

WE ARE THE AIR-SEA RESCUE

We are the Air-Sea Rescue,
No ruddy good are we.
The only time you'll find us
Is at breakfast, dinner, tea.
And when we see a dinghy
We shout with all our might,
" Per ardua Ad Astra—
Damn you, chaps, we're all right."

A song of 11 *Squadron which mixes the story of the squadron's travels with as much beer as can be obtained, adds an incident or two from squadron history, throws in a tot of Roll on the Boat for Home and serves with a dash of nostalgia to the tune of " Marching Through Georgia." Note: " Legs Eleven " is an expression from Housey-Housey, a harmless Service game permitted by Service Regulations, known otherwise as Tombola or Bingo.*

ROWS AND ROWS AND ROWS

We come from Legs Eleven, we're a shower of rotten skates,
We never pay the long-due rent and seldom pay the rates.
From the Nile to Singapore we've left our empty crates,
Laid out in rows and rows and rows.

> The beer, the beer, we don't drink lemon here,
> The beer, the beer, from Alex to Kashmir ;
> Bring your lovely barrels out and lay them down just here,
> Lay them out in rows and rows and rows.

Our officers are pilots of the very highest class,
Famous from Karachi up to the Kohat Pass,
They never use their undercarts, just lob 'em on the grass,
Lob 'em down in rows and rows and rows.

> The kites, the kites, the darlings of the flights,
> The kites, the kites, the fitters' joys, delights ;
> Push 'em into Servicing and we'll set 'em to rights
> And wheel 'em out in rows and rows and rows.

Our aircrews they just sit around in deck-chairs in the shade,
They never do a recco and they seldom do a raid,
But every Friday-fortnight when it's squadron pay parade
They're surging round in rows and rows and rows.

> Air Obs., Air Obs., to get their hard-earned bobs,
> A.G.s, A.G.s, they're milling round in threes ;
> Then back to the mess, you chaps, to lounge beneath the trees
> To get all drunk laid out in rows and rows.

We once lived in Elysian fields, as everybody knows,
Till one day came the Hurricanes with the yellow nose,
And Uncle Goering's little boys lashed out the daily dose,
Line astern in rows and rows and rows.

> The dives and loops they never seemed to shirk,
> We dug, deep down, and said, " God bless the work ! "
> They put the fear of you know what up every single erk
> Who grovelled there in rows and rows and rows.

We ended up in Palestine all dressed up in our rags,
With our trembling, twitching hands we lit our issue fags,
Took 211's ancient kites and duffed up the mags
And pushed them out in rows and rows and rows.

Oh what a hoot went up from old Beyrout,
Aleppo, too, got samples of the fruit,
The Berlin Travel Agency got shaken to the root
When their tourists tottered back in rows and rows.

When Raschid Ali hit the trail we graced the Mespot skies,
" The canteen's running out of beer " they told us 'tween their sighs ;
With little chitties that we forged we took them by surprise,
And they had to push it out in rows and rows.

Habbaniya's boys were shaken to the core,
The likes of us they'd never seen before ;
We left the Pro-hibition wallahs stretched upon the floor,
Then back across the Blue in rows and rows.

We all played snakes and ladders in the Western Desert " do,"
Dashing up and down and all around the flaming Blue,
And dear old Service Section had an awful lot to do,
Duff engines lining up in rows and rows.

Now old M'sus was never any use,
At Bu Amud the Jerries got too rude ;
Rommel's crafty recco showed we hadn't got it screwed,
So back to base in rows and rows and rows.

And now, my friends, it's fare-thee-well, I'm on the long-due boat,
I leave the squadron in Ceylon, a lump comes to my throat ;
But whatever Blighty squadron tries to get my goat,
We'll still have bottles there in rows and rows.

Wherever Legs Eleven tends to be,
They'll show them all a thing or two or three ;
And wherever there's a bottle or a *chota* drop of " ski "
You'll find the Eagles there in rows and rows.

SHE'S A SWELL DAME

Oh, she's plump and she's bon-nie to look at ___ An' I gaird her wi' in-fi-nite care ___ Yet her na-ture is such that it does na' tak' much To put her right up in the air. ___

Oh, she's plump an' she's bonnie to look at,
    An' I gaird her wi' infinite care,
Yet her nature is such that it doesna' tak' much
    To put her right up in the air.

She's the better class type, I may tell you—
    Though tellin' micht no' be the thing—
She's far, far abune me, an' folks whisper wi' glee,
    " He's got her, I hear, on a string."

But, believe me, I daw a' her sewin',
    It'll mak' her last longer, I hope,
An' I patiently wait if she's stayin' oot late,
    I aye gie her plenty o' rope.

There are times she's depressed an' collapsed,
    Oh, I dinna like seein' her doon,
But I dae what I can, an' it tak's a guid man,
    Tae attend tae a barrage balloon.

———

Sung by a balloon barrage squadron. 1942.   *To the tune of " It's Foolish,
But It's Fun."*

THE BALLOONATIC'S SONG

When civvy folk are tucked in tight,
And we are pushed on guard at night,
Although we know it isn't right,
It's foolish, but it's fun.

With whistles, truncheons, torches bright,
We march around the blooming site ;
Although we know it isn't right,
It's foolish, but it's fun.

We'd love to pull the rip line
And fire like bloomin' hell,
Then tell our officers and N.C.O.s
That they are fired as well.

We always see the morning light,
We work all day and guard all night,
Although we know it isn't right,
It's foolish, but it's fun.

In 1942 *the Liberators of* 511 *Squadron, Ferry Command, were flying cannon shells and fighter pilots into Malta during the seige, returning to Gibraltar without refuelling and with heavy loads of passengers aged from two weeks to ninety-two years. These aircraft had the then great range of* 3,700 *miles. The squadron also flew mail to Allied troops in North Africa in Albemarles— and for these they had no affection. To the tune of " Bless 'Em All."*

A LIB LEAVING MALTA FOR GIB

They say there's a Lib leaving Malta for Gib,
Heavier than ever before,
Tight to the turrets with terrified troops,
Fifty or sixty or more.
There's many a Hun with a gun in the sun
As they trundle back home to the Rock.
In case of brake failures they're glad of the Sailors
As they ditch at the end of the dock !

Chorus :   Five one one !   Five one one !
             From the snows to the sand and the sun.
             England to Cairo, and Bathurst to Hurn,
             All the world's records we prang 'em in turn.
             Over sea, over land,
             Through the ice and the *flak* and the sand,
             We're the kings of the air—Anytime, Anywhere—
             The Pride of Ferry Command.

There say there's an Albemarle down in the drink
Through a clot of a flight engineer,
She's been there for hours and still she won't sink
So they're sailing her on to Algier.
The Nav. and the Wop are both rowing like hell,
And the Co-pilot's setting the sails.
The kite is a bastard, the Skipper is plastered,
But he always delivers his mails !

Chorus

In November 1942 *the enemy took over Kairouan (or Qairwan), sacred city of Tunisia, after which the railway and adjacent airfields were subjected to Allied bombing till the city was taken by the British First Army five months later. This song originated with* 244 *or* 239 *Wing of the R.A.F. in the Western Desert at that time, its sentiments most appropriately set to the tune of " The Red Flag."*

TALES OF KAIROUAN

Now list to me and tales I'll tell of

Kai - rou - an, of Kai - rou - an, Your Spit - fire's just an

al - so ran, at Kai - rou - an, at Kai - rou - an, For

One - o - nines, and Focke-Wulfs too, are laugh - ing up their

sleeves at you, You have - n't got a firk - ing clue, at

Kai - rou - an, at Kai - rou - an.

Now list to me and tales I'll tell of Kairouan, of Kairouan,
Your Spitfires just an also-ran at Kairouan, at Kairouan.
For 109's, and Focke-Wulfs too, are laughing up their sleeves at you,
You haven't got a firking clue at Kairouan, at Kairouan.

I'll tell you tales of German *flak* at Kairouan, at Kairouan,
It comes up thick, it comes up black at Kairouan, at Kairouan.
You've only got a Spitfire V, so if you want to stay alive,
Press on the stick and dive and dive, and get away from Kairouan.

Sung slowly, morbidly.

And when this war is o'er and done at Kairouan, at Kairouan,
There'll be no Hun up in the Sun at Kairouan, at Kairouan,
So when again 'neath peaceful skies the Royal Air Force daily flies,
Think of the boy whose body lies at Kairouan, at Kairouan.

This song originated in 37 Squadron, 1940-41, and was characteristic of the spirit of bomber crews. The second line of verse three is a nice piece of work but, above all, the last verse is typical of the attitude of bomber boys returning from an operation, pestered on arrival by ground staff for their flimsies, pass and target maps. Sung to the hymn tune " Greenland's Icy Mountains " or " The Church's One Foundation."

THE HEAVY BOMBERS

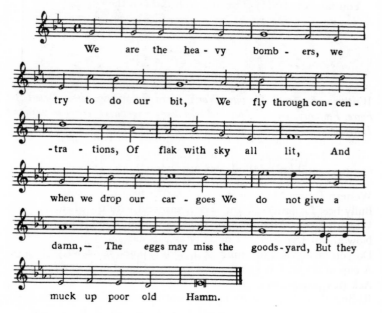

We are the heavy bombers, we try to do our bit,
   We fly through concentrations of flak with sky all lit,
And when we drop our cargoes, we do not give a damn,
   The eggs may miss the goods yard, but they muck up poor old Hamm.

And when in adverse weather the winds are all to hell,
   The navigator's balled up, the wireless balled as well,
We think of all the popsies we've known in days gone by,
   And curse the silly beggars who taught us how to fly.

They sent us out to Egypt, a very pleasant land,
   Where miles and miles of sweet dam-all are covered up with sand
And when we got to Cairo the girls were heard to say,
   " There ain't a hope for us, Dears, Thirty-seven's come to stay."

And in the Heavenly Ops Room, St. Peter will enquire,
" Did you cause an explosion or start a damn great fire? "
But when you see the angels tapping faultless morse,
You realise your Q.D.M. was a reciprocal course.

And if you go to Hades it's just like S.H.Q.,
There's lots of stooges sitting round with dam-all else to do,
They ask you for your flimsies, your pass and target maps,
You take the ruddy issue and stuff it down their traps.

---

*Written and sung at Martuta, North Africa, by 260 Squadron, Desert Air
Force, February, 1942. They had been doing magnificent service in worn-out
Hurricanes. To the tune of " South Sea Island Magic."*

WESTERN DESERT MADNESS

Western Desert Madness is caused by the heat of the sun,
Bully beef for breakfast and diceing around with the Hun.
Western Desert Madness has taken possession of me,
Now at last I've had it, I'm batty as bats can be.
Do you recall the crouching on a wadi exposed to view?
A cup of tea with benzine and a supper of hard tack stew?
Ack Ack, sandstorms, gremlins? But 260 still carries on,
Riding along the skyways in their worn-out Hurricanes One.

Western Desert Madness is caused by " that man again's " tact
For turning up at daybreak with orders for yet one more act.
Western Desert Madness has quite got this fine squadron's rag,
Thoughts of Oflag Nineteen, being captured and put in the bag.
Do you recall the straffing at Benina below the hill?
The Pongoes running madly, I bet they're beating it still !
Bad nights, Fanny, crack-ups? But 260 still make the grade
When Headquarters tell us to " get on with " a dawn straffing raid.

Western Desert Madness is caused by the Thirty Corps' flap,
Awkward situations and never being put on the map.
Western Desert Madness is caused by a lack of newspapers,
Stand-ups, Tac/R, Training and other impossible capers.
But we're resolved to stick it, and fight it out all on our own,
Despite what we've been promised such as Tomahawks given on loan,
Spitfires, Kitties, Typhoons are still as remote as the sun,
And we're *still* in the fore of the battle in our worn-out Hurricanes
One.

Sung by 605 *Squadron between November,* 1941, *and February,* 1942, *during the Battle of Malta. A typical squadron song, letting off steam in every line and exploding in all directions, conveying beautifully the spirit of the R.A.F. on operations. Note the similarity to " The Firth of Flaming Forth " page* 144 . *Sung to the tune of " John Brown's Body."*

A MALTA SONG

We're flying binding Hurricanes
  With binding long range tanks,
We do some aerobatics
  But we get no binding thanks.
But when we're coming home again
  We meet the binding Hun,
We press the binding button—
  It don't fire the binding gun.

Chorus: Ain't they binding lovely aircraft?
                   Ain't they binding lovely aircraft?
                   Ain't they binding lovely aircraft?
                   We press the binding button,
                   It don't fire the binding gun.

We're flying binding Wimpeys
  For miles and miles and miles,
It's not the ruddy distance, boys,
  But by Gort! my binding piles!
When we're coming home again
  At half-past binding six,
We prop our binding eyelids
  With sixteen binding sticks.

                   Ain't they binding lovely aircraft?
                   We prop our binding eyelids
                   With sixteen binding sticks.

We're flying binding Albacores
  At ninety-seven knots,
The engine's cutting out and
  Rattling off in binding spots.
We saw Castel Benito
  And dropped our binding bombs,
We made our binding landfall
  In a place called binding Homs.

                   Ain't they binding lovely aircraft?
                   We made our binding landfall
                   In a place called binding Homs.

We're flying binding Blenheims
  At masthead binding height,
Just to give the enemy
  A dirty binding fright.
And when we're coming home again
  We give a binding whoop,
We gun our binding motors
  And we do a binding loop.

Ain't they binding lovely aircraft?
We gun our binding motors
And we do a binding loop.

We're flying binding Ansons
  At 500 binding feet.
We fly them in the rain, the snow,
  And in the binding sleet.
And when we're flying south we find
  We're flying binding north,
And we make our binding landfall
  In the Firth of binding Forth.

Ain't they binding lovely aircraft?
We make our binding landfall
In the Firth of binding Forth.

We're flying binding Bostons
  At 250 binding feet,
Doing night intruders
  Just to see who we might meet.
And when the daylight dawns again
  And we can take a peek,
We find we've made our landfall
  Up the Clacton binding Creek.

Ain't they binding lovely aircraft?
We make our binding landfall
Up the Clacton binding Creek.

We're flying binding Whitleys
  At 90 miles per hour,
Browned-off binding pilots
  Feeling kinda sour,
But the tail-end binding Charlie
  Thinks it's all a binding treat:
To shoot the binding Hun, says he,
  Is easy binding meat.

Ain't they binding lovely aircraft?
To shoot the binding Hun, says he,
Is easy binding meat.

The Compiler apologises for the inclusion of this song (his own) but waives his modesty on the grounds that it does give a fair picture of the kind of things that happened on newly-opened R.A.F. stations. It was written and sung in 1941 and 1942, and appeared in the " Royal Air Force Quarterly." Music of the chorus is original but verse goes to the tune " My Name is Solomon Levi."

A SONG OF 51 MAINTENANCE UNIT

No - vem - ber, nine - teen thir - ty - nine: Near three-spired(censored) town— They start - ed ex - ca - va - ting land And whack-ing con - crete down.— The res - i - dent en - gi - neer worked hard, They dug out holes and cra - ters,— They lev - elled out wide mead - ows, Sowed grass where once grew 'ta-ters. Strong armed con-trac - tors hauled and hacked, They sawed and cut and bored,— They built our mas - sive han - gars where Win - ston's air - craft's stored.— The months went by and fin - al - ly (their ef - forts un - dim - in - ished) for oc - cu - pa - tion by the Raf the place (they claimed) was fin - ished.

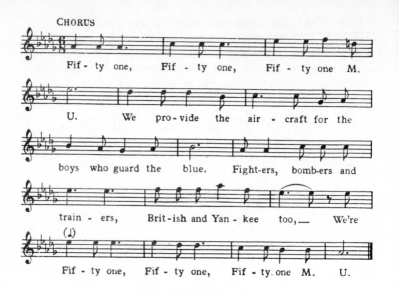

CHORUS

Fif - ty one, Fif - ty one, Fif - ty one M.
U. We pro - vide the air - craft for the
boys who guard the blue. Fight-ers, bomb-ers and
train - ers, Brit -ish and Yan - kee too, — We're
Fif - ty one, Fif - ty one, Fif - ty. one M. U.

November Nineteen-Thirty-Nine:
Near three-spired (censored) town
They started excavating land
And whacking concrete down.
The Resident Engineer worked hard,
They dug out holes and craters,
They levelled out wide meadows,
Sowed grass where once grew taters.
Strong-armed contractors hauled and hacked,
They sawed and cut and bored,
They built our massive hangars
Where Winston's aircraft's stored.
The months went by and finally
(Their efforts undiminished)
For occupation by the R.A.F.
The place (they claimed) was finished.

    Chorus :
        Fifty-one, Fifty-one, Fifty-one M.U.
        We provide the aircraft
        For the boys who guard the blue.
        Fighters, bombers and trainers,
        British and Yankee too,
        We're Fifty-one, Fifty-one, Fifty-one M.U.

When July, Nineteen-Forty, came
The Unit was inspected.
" This station isn't ready yet,"
Said C.O. sore dejected.

The aerodrome was half complete,
The hangars had no doors,
The M.T. yard was just a field,
The guard-room had no floors.
The huts were mere flat sections,
The roads a complete sell,
The Institute was hardly built,
And Workshops was a shell.
But A.O.C. said, " Do your best,"
And C.O. said, " Quit slacking,
We're going to turn out aircraft now,
Come on, you chaps, get cracking."

So August, Nineteen-Forty, saw
Us open up the show.
We read our names in P.O.R.'s
And Orders, D.R.O.
But boy ! it was an uphill job !
We raised demands galore,
But no one seemed to fill them,
They'd nothing in the store.
The stationery failed to come,
Defence had rifles nil,
We were routed via Hampshire,
The tea was just like swill.
The heating wouldn't work at all,
The roads were full of ruts,
The sanitation let us down,
And so did Five Site's huts.

Dispersal guards collapsed at nights,
The Adjutant saw red,
The Engineering Officer
Shot Chiefies in their bed.
The drome became a foggy lake,
The runways far from level,
The pilots landed upside down,
Padre embraced the devil.
The orderly room ran out of forms,
The mess ran out of bread,
We had no soap, we had no cheese,
The 'lectric light was dead.
And then some Polish airmen came,
They could not speak so good,
The only words they understood
Were " Pay parade " and " food."

Tin hats and tool kits we had none,
The cooks were plagued with mice,
The washing always came back late,
And ants consumed the rice.
One week the snow came down so fast
It stood feet deep in slush,
We had no plough to clear the drome
And had to use a brush.
We seemed to spend the whole long day
Hauling planes for miles
Across ten-thousand-acre fields
And sometimes over stiles.
The M.O. dosed us all with rum,
Feared for our future health,
He 'noculated all the lot,
And then went sick himself.

By spring we all felt well nigh dead,
But now we had won through,
And Fifty-one was doing its stuff,
For the boys who guard the blue.
The hangars all hummed busily,
The Stores were full of gear,
Sick Quarters all looked spick and span,
We thrived on Burton's beer.
Thus through the winter's cold and mud
And ice and sleet and snowing,
Four hundred airmen gave their sweat
To get this station going.
So don't forget those early days
(the point of this oration) :
Those airmen suffered bloody hell
To open up this station.   So—
        Fifty-one, Fifty-one, Fifty-one M.U.
        We provide the aircraft
        For the boys who guard the blue.
        Fighters, bombers and trainers,
        British and Yankee too.
        We're Fifty-one, Fifty-one, Fifty-one M.U.

Sung by 70 Squadron, 1941-42, during the Libyan Campaign, when their bombing of Benghazi was so regular they called it a mail run. Fuka was an aerodrome, 60 and 09 were landing grounds. Sung to the tune of "Clementine."

THE BENGHAZI MAIL RUN

Take off for the Western Desert,
    Fuka, 60 or 09,
Same old Wimpey, same old target,
    Same old aircrew, same old time.

Chorus: Seventy Squadron, Seventy Squadron,
           Though we say it with a sigh,
           Must we do this ruddy mail run
           Every night until we die?

Navigator, have you lost us?
    Come up here and have a look.
Someone's shot our starboard wing off,
    That's alright, then, that's Tobruk.

Forty Wimpeys on the target,
    Two were ditched down in the drink,
Then three others crashed on landing,
    Bloomin' hell! it makes you think.

Stooging round the Western Desert
  With the gravy running low,
How I wish I could see Fuka
  Through the sandstorm down below.

First it's Derna, then it's Barce,
  Even I.O. isn't sure—
They've changed the bomb loads twice already,
  It's a proper Cookie's Tour.

All this flapping cannot fool us,
  We know just where we'll have to be,
Rumour's heard of a new target,
  But after all it's just B.G.

To Benghazi is the slogan,
  We'll take the load right through once more,
So start your engines, let's get cracking,
  The mail run's going as before.

'Telligence tells us from his photos
  We never hit a single flea,
Sees no bomb holes in the rooftops,
  Only craters in the sea.

He asks us if we're " sure we pranged it? "
  Must have been some other spot,
Suggests we bombed a dummy target,
  Never heard such utter clot !

Try to get your tour of ops in
  Without your aircraft being hit.
If you do you'll go to Blighty,
  If you don't you're in the pit.

Oh to be in Piccadilly
  Selling matches by the score !
Though we'd feel a little chilly,
  There'd be no mail run any more.

A song sung by a fighter station's ground staff, 1942. To the tune of " She'll be coming Round the Mountain."

A SERVICING SONG

She'll be skid-ding down the run-way when she

comes, She'll be skidding down the run-way when she

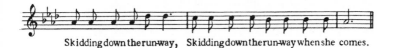

comes, She'll be skid-ding down the run-way,

Skidding down the run-way, Skidding down the run-way when she comes.

CHORUS

Sing - ing I, I, yip - py yip - py

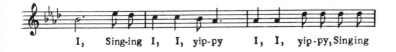

I, Sing-ing I, I, yip - py yip - py

I, Sing-ing I, I, yip-py I, I, yip-py, Singing

I, I, yip-py yip-py I.

193

She'll be skidding down the runway when she comes,
She'll be skidding down the runway when she comes,
She'll be skidding down the runway,
She'll be skidding down the runway,
She'll be skidding down the runway when she comes.

Chorus :   Singing I, I Yippy Yippy I,
              Singing I, I Yippy Yippy I,
              Singing I, I Yippy, I, I Yippy,
              Singing I, I Yippy, Yippy I.

She'll be needin' ammunition when she comes, etc.

She'll be thirstin' for more gravy when she comes, etc.

She'll be smothered up with glycol when she comes, etc.

She'll be weepin' tears of oil when she comes, etc.

She'll be plugged chock full of holes when she comes, etc.

She'll be short of a propeller when she comes, etc.

She'll be minus both her engines when she comes, etc.

She'll be rudderless and flapless when she comes, etc.

She'll be tailless, she'll be wingless, when she comes, etc.

She'll be needin' fitters 'n' riggers when she comes, etc.

But she'll bring back her driver when she comes, etc.

He'll have plenty in the bag when he comes, etc.

He'll be yearning for his popsie when he comes, etc.

AS YOU BED YOUR BALLOON IN THE MORNING

D'ye ken B. I. on a rain - y night When the

mud's so thick that the site's out of sight? When the

tac-kle's un-der wa-ter How the hell d'ye take a bight? When you

bed your bal - loon in the morn - ing.

CHORUS

'Twas the sound of the 'phone brought me

from my bed And a well - known voice from Op - er -

- a - tions said, There's light-ning re - port - ed from

Bir - ken - head, Bed down for a thun-der storm warn - ing.

D'ye ken B.1 on a rainy night,
When the mud's so thick that the site's out of sight?
When the tackle's under water, how the hell d'you take a bight?
When you bed your balloon in the morning.

Chorus: 'Twas the sound of the phone brought me from my bed,
            And a well-known voice from Operations said,
            " There's lightning reported from Birkenhead—
            Bed down for a thunderstorm warning."

D'ye ken B.2 when the wind blows keen,
And the ruddy old balloon looks most obscene,
And the surge drums are covered with lanoline
As you bed your balloon in the morning.

D'ye ken B.3 when the chimneys spark?
Have you ever changed a bed there after dark?
Well, it's solid ruddy rock in St. George's Park,
As you bed your balloon in the morning.

Then there's B.16 when the wind is in the East,
And the b'loon yaws about like a wounded beast,
And the cable kinks even though it's been greased,
As you bed your balloon in the morning.

Then there's S.17 which is quite a good site,
Though its crew always seems a little bit tight,
'Cos they never get their hydrogen report quite right,
As they bed their balloon in the morning.

Now I dreamt one night that the war had been won,
And " B " Flight had brought down the last ruddy Hun,
And I said to myself, " My God, what fun !
We can all go back home in the morning."

And I can say, " Blast that telephone bell,"
And the well-known voice can go to—well,
You know what I mean so what the hell !
But I woke from my dream in the morning.

Sung by a station concert party in 1942 *at a technical training school, The phrase " You've had it " means " You've missed it," and is full-blooded R.A.F. A pretty lyric, by Flying Officer Arthur Macrae, who also wrote " There's No A.M.O. About Love " (page* 201).

YOU'VE HAD IT

1st Verse:

There is a phrase, that seems to haunt my days,
Since I was just a sprog, my footsteps it has seemed to dog,
If I want jam—or just a spot more ham,
Somebody's bound to shout,
" You've 'ad it, luv,"
Although I've not had nowt.

1st Chorus:

When first of all I joined the Waafs,
My goodness, I was daft,
At Gloucester in the cookhouse,
Well, you really would have laughed,
I beckoned to an officer who came inspecting teas,
And said, " I don't like eggs, so can I see the menu, please? "
I thought he hadn't understood—he looked a bit pop-eyed—
I added nicely, " Just some fish would do—if lightly fried."
He gasped, he choked, went purple—then most rudely he replied,
" You've 'ad it."

2nd Verse:

I love my work, and seldom ever shirk,
I make balloons all day, which as you know is madly gay,
But sure as Fate—if I want one pass, late,
They say, " You've 'ad it, dear,
You're duty washer-up tonight, I fear."

2nd Chorus:

I wonder just who started up this binding little phrase?
Did Gladstone say, " You've 'ad it, chum " in Queen Victoria's
    days?
It's very, very catching, and I know it's going to spread,
They'll get it soon in Hollywood, and that's a thing I dread.
When Garbo's clasped in Gable's arms, just at the close of day
He'll whisper low, " Be mine tonight — tomorrow, come what
    may,"
She'll sigh, and smile a little, then look up at him and say,
" You've 'ad it."

I'm going to be married soon, the groom's an L.A.C.
Me bottom drawer is crammed with really lovely lingerie.
I've got me man, I've got me dress, I've everything it seems,
But somehow I am haunted by the nastiest kind of dreams :
I'm in the Church, all hopeful-like, and then get filled with doubt,
And just as all me lilies wilt, and I'm near passing out,
The Vicar and the congregation all get up and shout,
" You've 'ad It ! "

A song-parody written for and sung by a station concert party. The Service policeman is a standard R.A.F. butt for humour, and he takes it very well. Sung to the tune of Offenbach's "The Gendarmes' Duet."

A SERVICE POLICE SONG

We're Service Policemen bold and wary,
   And of ourselves we take good care ;
To risk our precious lives we're chary,
   When danger looms we're never there.
But when we meet a helpless airman
Or little Waaf out on the spree—
     We run 'em in, we run 'em in, we run 'em in,
     We run 'em in, we show them we're the bold S.P.

And if their hair's not short and beautiful,
   Or they're not back in time from leave,
If they're unairmanlike, undutiful,
   If they do hardly more than breathe,
We slap 'em on a Two-Five-Two, Sir,
And get 'em jankers and C.C.—
     We run 'em in, we show them we're the bold S.P.

If boisterous airmen make a riot,
   Or drink down too much beer at night,
We're quite disposed to keep it quiet
   Providing that we too get tight.
But if they do not seem to see it
Or stand us all our proper fee—
     We run 'em in, we show them we're the bold S.P.

Sometimes our snooping's off the camp, Sir,
   When wicked airmen we pursue,
We pinch the types who don't salute, Sir,
   And shake the other types who do.
Unto our police posts back returning,
To make ourselves a pot of tea—
     We run 'em in, we show them we're the bold S.P.

Written and sung at the School of Royal Air Force Administration ; most war-time adjutants and administrative officers underwent a course there at some time or another. 1942. Sung to the tune of " The Vicar of Bray."

SO HERE I WORK

An A. M. sig-nal spoiled my joy Way back on a rud-dy good sta-tion— "Off on a course you'll go, my boy, To learn ad-min-is-tra-tion." I packed a bag and caught a cab, And dashed off to the sta-tion, And why I— nev-er missed that train, Is past im-ag-in-a-tion.

CHORUS

So here I work and some-times play, But nev-er bill and coo, sir, And if on this sta-tion I must stay, I'll re-mus-ter to A. C. 2.— sir!

An A.M. signal spoiled my joy
    Way back on a ruddy good station—
" Off on a course you'll go, my boy,
    To learn Administration."
I packed a bag and caught a cab,
    And dashed off to the station,
And why I never missed that train
    Is past imagination.

Chorus :   So here I work and sometimes play,
            But never bill and coo, Sir,
            And if on this station I must stay
            I'll remuster to A.C.2, Sir.

This station's such a great big place
    With lots of sleeping huts, Sir :
Get up early, rush for food,
    Have mercy on our guts, Sir.
A rissole is their favourite dish,
    And kipper their only fish, Sir,
But when this ruddy war is done
    I'll stick to bacon and eggs, Sir.

They say the Waafs—some thirty strong—
    Are full of oomph and glamour,
But when they're in the lecture room
    They just stand up and stammer.
When to the town nearby we go
    (Assuming we all get transport)
Some thirty blokes (not me or you)
    Provide them with an escort.

Our lecturers are noble men,
    They help us all they can, Sir,
K.R.'s and A.M.O.'s they read,
    We quote them in our sleep, Sir.
'Tis said that some of us will stay
    To be a swell Admin. reader,
If only a monocle I could wear
    I'd soon be a Squadron Leader.

Written by Flying Officer Arthur Macrae for a station concert party in 1942, *subsequently broadcast by the B.B.C. in R.A.F. programmes and sung in many Service shows. When included in an R.A.F. revue at the Phœnix Theatre, London, the* Daily Sketch *described it as " the wittiest of several witty enough for inclusion in any West End revue." The verse is done as a monologue.*

THERE'S NO A.M.O. ABOUT LOVE

Sir Archibald—I really am in quite a shocking flap,
So will you, just for my sake, be an awfully decent chap.
You see, Sir A., the trouble's really this, I have a girl,
And what with this and that she's got me into quite a whirl.
Now you, and several other blokes, as everybody knows,
Think up those helpful little pamphlets known as A.M.O.s,
But *honestly*, Sir Archibald, there's something gravely lacking,
So will you call a conference and get your chappies cracking?

Chorus:

There's no A.M.O. about love,
You've missed out nothing else from rats to rations ;
But I've searched for days and days
Through the " N's " and through the " A's "
And I can't find any ruling on the tender passions.
There's advice on bites of tse-tse flies in most peculiar places,
What not to say if A.O.C.s produce more than four aces,
And there's how to serve spaghetti to a sheikh in an oasis,
But there's no A.M.O. about love.

I'm sure you'll see the danger, sir, we all go off on leave,
So many of us, young, untried, unsullied and naive.
We're lured by siren voices and we finish up as wrecks,
At the mercy of what laughingly is called the weaker sex.
So I suggest an A.M.O., and please don't think it cheek,
On " Love—And All About It "—with appendix on Technique.
Or p'raps you could amend K.R.s, they need a bit of checking,
Insert a Para somewhere on the gentle art of necking.

Chorus:

There's no A.M.O. about love,
You really must admit it's rather stupid,
There are several slightly odd
Little hints on salted cod,
There are lots and lots on swill, but not a thing on Cupid.
There's one on station libraries, and two on station cats,
A slightly nauseating one on un-cooked mutton fats,
There's what to do with gas-capes, and what not to do with A.T.S.
But there's no A.M.O. about love.

There's no A.M.O. about love,
There's gardening, and garbage pails—and E.N.S.A.,
But if someone waves a wand,
And you meet a lovely blonde,
Oh what to do, and when, and where—there's not a scrap of gen, sir.
You burst into her boudoir, and she's looking simply great,
You say " My darling Love "—and see the other chap too late,
And she says, " My husband's home on unexpected forty-eight,"
There's no A.M.O. about love.

There's one on boots knee rubber, and there's one on ale and stout,
Some *splendid* sanitation hints on types inside and out,
And there's how to bed a mule down in the Orkneys in a drought,
But there's no A.M.O. about love.

———————

From a 1943 *concert party show by No.* 1 *Squadron, commemorating the
lady—familiar on most stations—who toured around the dispersal areas in a
mobile van providing tea, cakes and (if you were lucky) cigarettes. By
Corporal J. Holdsworth.*

MRS. MOBILE

They call her Mrs. Mobile,
And her dial's familiar,
Around the perim
              —around the perim.
And everybody knows her,
Each airman " Hello's " her,
Though she don't know him
              —though she don't know him.
Around the dispersals she travels each day,
She needs no rehèarsal for she knows her way.
And there's a lot of gen she learns from what the airmen say
While she's mobile in her mobile.

Typical bomber squadron song, inspired by the popularity of Miss Cicely Courtneidge's " The King's Horses, The King's Men " to the tune of which it of course went.

FIFTY ONE SQUADRON

Chorus : Fifty-one Squadron, Fifty-one Men,
Fly over Germany and fly back again,
Fifty-one Squadron, Fifty-one Men.

They're not there to fight the foe,
You might think so, but Oh Dear No,
They're just there to have a go
And put a bit of action in the Goering show.
They fly in Whitley's big and black,
And all think that they're the ones who're coming back,
Fifty-one Squadron, Fifty-one Men.

Chorus : They fly at night-time, they fly by day,
But when there's a clamp on then it's Boys come Out to
Play,
Fifty-one Squadron, Fifty-one Men.

Fifty-one Squadron, Fifty-one Men,
Fly over Germany and fly back again,
Fifty-one Squadron, Fifty-one Men.

Sung by a detachment of the Women's Division (" Wids ") of the Royal Canadian Air Force, 1942-43, London, to the tune of " I am the Ruler of the Queen's Navee," from " H.M.S. Pinafore."

THE WIDS' SONG

In war-torn England there was great demand
For loyal women who could lend a hand.
They needed some girls to help the RAF,
So they formed an Auxiliary and called it WAAF.
They did their job so efficiently
That soon there were units through the whole country.

Their fame it spread through the Empire wide
Across the sea to the Canadian side.
We called on the Waaf to come to our aid,
They sent four officers and plans were laid.
And so we got the Wids under way
Without any trouble and with little delay.

We learned to drill, to do P.T.,
To stand the shock of T.A.B.T.
We studied the laws of organisation,
K.R. and administration.
We finished our course with a great parade
And were posted away to practise our trade.
And then one day it happened to us,
Without any bother and without much fuss,
That off to England we should go
To lend a hand in this goldarn show,
And are we glad to be here too,
Just watch us swagger in the Air Force blue.

So hand in hand and side by side
The Waafs and Wids will turn the tide.
We'll lick the German, beat the Jap,
We'll wipe them off the blinkin' map,
We hope our loyal service will be
A boost to the ultimate Victory.

A typical bomber squadron song. For the uninitiated, it should be explained that the verses are written in pseudo-dialogue form as a conversation might take place by radio telephone between aircraft eager to land and the Operations Room on the ground. Sung to the tune of " Clementine."

A 218 SQUADRON SONG

At the Bea - con, at the Bea - con, Land-ing turn is num-ber nine, And the air - craft all are say - ing, "One more hour and I've had mine."

CHORUS

O'er the Bea - con, o'er the Bea - con, can you hear our mel - o - dy? Get - ting hours in, get - ting hours in, Just two hun - dred hours for me.

At the beacon, at the beacon,
Landing turn is Number 9,
And the aircraft are all saying,
" One more hour and I've had mine."

Chorus: O'er the beacon, o'er the beacon,
Can you hear our melody?
Getting hours in, getting hours in,
Just 200 hours for me.

They are calling, they are calling,
They are calling to us all.
So we switch the TR9 on
And the answer is " Dam-all."

Comes a fighter, comes a fighter,
Comes a Junkers 88.
" Hurry, Archie, hurry, Archie,
Or you'll be too bleedin' late."

" Hello Darkie, hello Darkie,
　　There's a fighter giving chase,
Hello Darkie, hello Darkie,
　　Where the hell's the course for base? "

" Hello aircraft, hello aircraft,
　　What's it got to do with me?
Circle beacon, circle beacon,
　　Q.F.E. is 923 ! "

" Hellow Archie, hello Archie,
　　Aircraft's shooting hard at me."
" Hello aircraft, hello aircraft,
　　Shoot it down," says P.A.D.

" Hello Archie, hello Archie,
　　We've received and understood,
Remove fingers remove fingers,
　　Blighter's down in Old Monk's Wood."

" Hello Archie, hello Archie,
　　Can I now come in and land? "
" Hello aircraft, hello aircraft,
　　Would you like the ruddy band? "

" Hello aircraft, hello aircraft,
　　Get a green when you are near."
" Hello Archie, hello Archie,
　　I have left the flare-path clear."

To the Ops Room, to the Ops Room,
　　From dispersal we must go.
What the hell's gone wrong with transport?
　　Lord Almighty, aren't they slow?

We are down, Sir, we are down, Sir,
　　And no thanks to Sentinel 2.
Our results, Sir, thanks to Met., Sir,
　　Our results we leave to you.

A pretty little bomber song sung by 175 and other Squadrons in 1942 to the tune of "My Bonnie."

BRING BACK MY BOMBER AND ME

One night as I lay on my pillow,
  My batman awoke me and said,
" I say, there are ships in the Channel,
  But there's bags of black cloud overhead."
Chorus: Bring back, bring back, bring back my bomber and me,
  Bring back, bring back, bring back my bomber and me.

So I climbed in my old heavy bomber,
  And I took off right dead into wind,
And I searched the whole of the Channel,
  But not a damn ship could I find.
      Bring back, bring back, bring back my bomber and me,
      Bring back, bring back, bring back my bomber and me.

207

So I turned round and headed for England,
  Just thinking of coffee and bed,
The Controller said, " How come you missed them? "
  And I leave you to guess what I said.
        Bring back, bring back, bring back my bomber and me,
        Bring back, bring back, bring back my bomber and me.

Concert party song about the ground servicing crews, 1943. *By Corporal
J. Holdsworth.*

THE FITTER, THE RIGGER, THE MECH

We're the men who put the kites in the air,
We're the guys who keep them under repair.
The Fitter, the Rigger, the Mech,
The fellows who work on the deck ;
The Butcher, the Baker, the Instrument-maker,
The " Plumber," 'lectrician, and Tyre-pressure-taker.
But no one ever sings our praises in song,
What we do ain't noticed till it goes wrong !
We don't get the medals, the credit, the kudos, the girls or front
    seats at the Show ;
But where would the pilots, observers and gunners be, we're anxious
    to know,
Without the airmen who put the kites in the air?

Chant:
I'm the fitter—the rigger—the " plumber "—
Who put the kite in the air.
I'm the store-basher—
I'm the cook who clothe and feed
The fitter—the rigger—the " plumber "
Who put the kite in the air.
I'm the A.C.H./G.D. who opens the cases and peels the spuds for
    the—
Basher and cook
Who clothe and feed
The fitter—the rigger—the " plumber "
Who put the kite in the air.
I'm the driver who brings the goods at a limiting speed of 20 miles
    for the—
A.C.H. who opens the cases and peels the spuds for the—
Basher and cook
Who clothe and feed
The fitter—the rigger—the " plumber "
Who put the kite in the air.
Yes !

This song originated at Cranwell in about 1942 *and was later sung on Royal Canadian Air Force and other stations.*

ONCE THERE WAS A NAAFI GIRL

Once there was a Naafi Girl
    And she was dressed in blue, Sir,
And in her little Institute
    She kept a bomber crew, Sir.
She kept a bomber crew, my lads,
    And kept the camp alive-o,
And when she shouted " Contact ! "
    All the bombers had to dive-o.

She said to Skipper Bill one day,
    " O come now will you fly me
Upon an operation in
    Your Wimpey o'er the high sea? "
" It's right against K.R.," said he,
    " But for you I will risk it—
You'd better make your will right now—
    My Love, you take the biscuit."

So then our little Naafi Girl
    Dressed herself in brown, Sir,
Administered a spot of rouge
    And took her face to town, Sir.

209

She loaded up her mobile van
   With tea and buns all ready,
And drove out to dispersal
   To the Wimpey " F " for Freddie.

She then filled up the kite with wads
   And urns of Naafi tea, Sir,
She stored them all away in there
   As neatly as could be, Sir.
And then she put her greatcoat on
   (Careful of her kitting),
She hid herself in the fuselage
   And passed the time by knitting.

Soon Skipper Bill and all his crew
   Arrived out on dispersal.
They'd done their N.F.T. that morn
   And needed no rehearsal.
The kite took off right merrily,
   All bombed up and quite slick-o,
And when they reached the open sea
   Our Naafi Girl was sick-o.

But she'd recovered by the time
   They reached their destined target,
Though it did not remind her of
   A pleasure trip to Margate.
The flak came up as thick as mud,
   They'd got the range for certain,
And if Bill hadn't kept his head
   That Wimpey'd gone for a Burton.

Our Naafi Girl then did her stuff,
   Inspired by the Gods, Sir,
She jettisoned the urns of tea
   And started dropping wads, Sir.
Right o'er the target they went down,
   Into the fires all burning,
And she'd released the whole darn lot
   When the kite was homeward turning.

That target looked like hell let loose,
   She'd pranged it off the map, Sir,
The flames roared up from the black below,
   She'd given it the strap, Sir.
Explosions threw the kite about,
   They'd blown up the whole place, Sir.
And when Bill saw what she had done.
   He set the course for base, Sir.

Now none else knows about this spree,
   Of that there is no doubt, Sir.
But honestly I've told you how
   That target was wiped out, Sir.
The boys all got the D.F.C.,
   And the Naafi Girl was wed-o
To Bill the valiant skipper
   Of the Wimpey " F " for Fred-o.

A Coastal squadron song, written in 1942 *by the orderly room staff—Corporal
Mack, L.A.C. Dobbing, L.A.C. Hemsley and L.A.C. Smith. It does not
grouse, as so many squadron songs do, but boasts of the squadron's exploits.
Verse to the tune of " My Bonnie Lies Over the Ocean " and chorus to
" Elmer's Tune."*

A SONG OF 59 SQUADRON

A squadron swept over the ocean,
A squadron swept over the sea,
They chased the Hun back to his harbours,
Now who could that darned squadron be?

Chorus:
Who makes the Hun send his convoys out only at night?
Or when the fogs and the clouds hide the blighters from sight?
And makes them scatter and shiver and tremble with fright?
   It's Just 59 !
What makes old Hitler feel littler with each passing day?
It's just the worry and flurry of us in his way,
What makes old Goering go roaring and say he won't play?
   It's Just 59 !
Bombing shipping, everybody thinks it's simply ripping !
Turning, diving—" Look out for that mast or it may be your last ! "
So when you hear on the news that a boat has been sunk,
And Jerry's ships are reduced to a load of old junk,
You can be sure that the aircrews whose health will be drunk.
   Come from 59 !

A squadron swept over the ocean,
Their aircraft must airworthy be,
They're kept in that state by the ground-crews,
Now who could those fine fellows be?

Who does the work on the engines all hours of the day?
And patches the airframe when it's shot away?
And tunes up the kites so they're fit for the fray?
   Flight Mechs 59 !
Who puts the bombs on the racks when we go on a raid?
And sees that the ammo has not been mislaid ?

And checks the guns and the turrets until they're O.K.'d ?
    Armourers 59 !
Tuning, testing, working all the time and never resting,
Fitters, riggers, tightening the screws that'll make the Huns lose,
And who D.I. the S.E. and are always discreet?
And make of the circuits and wiring a feat?
Who brings the planes back to base when the raid is complete?
    Signals 59 !
Bombing shipping, everybody thinks it's simply ripping,
Turning, diving, " Look out for that mast or it may be your last ! "
So when you hear on the news that a boat has been sunk,
And Jerry's ships are reduced to a load of old junk,
You can be sure that the aircrews whose health will be drunk
    Come from 59 !

Sung in station concert party shows, 1943, and reflecting the airman's deep interest in and love for physical training. By Corporal J. Holdsworth.

EVERYBODY'S CRACKERS ON P.T.

Around the perimeter we've gotta run,
And the reason for it's very plain to see :
We've got to run until we're fit to drop !
'Cos everybody's crackers on P.T.
Bar Me !
Outside the hangar when duty is done
There's an eager rush to form up into three.
We love the running when it's time to stop !
'Cos everybody's crackers on P.T.
Each puffing airman, as the others dash past,
Puts a little spurt on, swears he won't be last.
Each binding corporal, when his wind's getting short,
Underneath his breath says things he didn't ought !
Sergeants and officers, corporals and erks
Love to stand around dispersal to see—
Boots, Boots, Boots, Boots, movin' up and down again—
'Cos everybody's crackers on P.T.
Bar Me ! !

In the R.A.F. the flight mechanic is the fitter's mate—he is the humblest of the technical ground staff. This song is to the tune of perhaps the most "stolen" hymn of all, 1942. "The Church's One Foundation" or "Greenland's Icy Mountains."

THE FLIGHT MECHANIC'S SONG

Lords of the air, they call us, They voice our grow-ing fame: The front page of each pa - per A - dorned with a pi - lot's name. In sto-ries of deeds of va - lour In - scribed up in the sky, You read of high-speed bat - tles Fought by the men who fly.

Lords of the Air, they call us,
    They voice our growing fame :
The front page of each paper
    Adorned with a pilot's name.
In stories of deeds of valour
    Inscribed up in the sky,
You read of high-speed battles
    Fought by the men who fly.

There's one who gets no medals,
    You never hear his name,
He does not fly in the pale blue sky
    Nor pose for the News with a plane,
His job ain't called romantic
    Or one for public gaze ;
But the Lords of the Air respect him
    And often give him praise.

Who inspects the kite each morning?
  Who fills up the tanks each night?
Who keeps the engines always sweet?
  Who keeps the pressure right?
Who's up at crack of dawning?
  Still there as twilight fades?
Who pulls his weight to keep the crate
  All set to make its raids?

When next you see a picture
  Of plane and smiling crew,
Recall the bloke who keeps it there
  Who's only an A.C.2.
Next time you praise a pilot
  As Jerry falls a wreck,
Remember the guy who doesn't fly—
  The humble, proud Flight Mech.

Written and sung at the School of Royal Air Force Administration, 1942.
*The words are by Courtney Hume to music by Gordon Brand. Done in the
style of the Western Brothers.*

IT'S LAID DOWN

Now I'm a bloke from the Admin. School
Where we're officers and gents,
Although I've only half a ring
I think that I'm immense.
I'm up here on an Admin. Course,
I'm here to do my stuff,
Although I've learnt a little
It's not nearly half enough.

  It's laid down, yes, it's laid down,
  I've seen it in K.R.s, it's laid down.
  I saw a student officer entertain a student Waaf,
  I know it's very rude of me, I couldn't help but laff,
  I thought that all the glamour girls were signed up by the staff ;
  It's in K.R.s, it's laid down.

At question time the other day,
A Waaf, a vulgar gal,
Said, " How do you spell ' closet ' ?
Tell me teacher, be a pal."
He said, " My Dear, that's easy,
Spell it L A V A L—
It's in K.R.s, it's laid down."

I saw the Messing Officer
Right past the Guard Room steal
He crept across the golf links,
Believe me, his stealth was real,
He was on his way to a hotel
Trying to get a decent meal—
It's in K.R.s, it's laid down.

It's laid down, yes, it's laid down,
I've seen it in K.R.s, it's laid down.
This station is the place in which we learn air force careers,
They guarantee to teach you your Admin. without the tears,
We've one bloke in our syndicate who's been here 20 years—
It's in K.R.s, it's laid down.

A bloke from an asylum
Got in here the other day,
No one recognised him,
Not a soul would say him nay,
He took all examinations
And he passed out with an "A,"
It's in K.R.s, it's laid down.

At discussion time of strolls outside
We're told there can't be any,
We can only talk of Admin.,
Not of Garbo or Jack Benny,
The only way to get a smoke
Is to go and spend a penny—
It's in K.R.s, it's laid down.

It's laid down, yes, it's laid down,
I've seen it in K.R.s, it's laid down.
The Brains Trust came up here, old fruit, to learn the Admin.
    code,
Now they know all the answers and we're on the right road
'Cos Wing Commander Sullock's really dear Professor Joad—
It's in K.R.s, it's laid down.

We're giving Nazi Germany
A good old Raf what-for,
We've finished dropping leaflets
And we're dropping bombs and more—
On Adolf Hitler's birthday
We dropped " The Manual of Air Force Law,"
It's in K.R.s, it's laid down.

YOU'LL NEVER GO TO HEAVEN

You'll never go to Heaven in a Hurricane One,
You'll stall before your journey's done,
O! you'll never go to Heaven in a Hurricane One,
You'll stall before your journey's done,
I ain't a'gonna grieve my Lord no more.

Chorus: I ain't a'gonna grieve my Lord no more,
          I ain't a'gonna grieve my Lord no more,
          I ain't a'gonna grieve my Lord no more.

You'll never get to Heaven if you're flying Spits,
The Lord don't want no clever twits,
O! you'll never go to Heaven if you're flying Spits,
The Lord don't want no clever twits,
I ain't a'gonna grieve my Lord no more.

You'll never get to Heaven in a Deffy Two,
You ought to see the glycol spew,
O! you'll never go to Heaven in a Deffy Two,
You ought to see the glycol spew,
I ain't a'gonna grieve my Lord no more.

You'll never get to Heaven in a Martinet,
At least no blighter's done it yet,
O! you'll never go to Heaven in a Martinet,
At least no blighter's done it yet,
I ain't a'gonna grieve my Lord no more.

You'll never get to Heaven in a Master Three,
It couldn't even climb a tree,
O! you'll never get to Heaven in a Master Three,
It couldn't even climb a tree,
I ain't a'gonna grieve my Lord no more.

You'll never get to Heaven in a woman's arms,
'Cos de Lord don't like dem feminine charms,
O! you'll never get to Heaven in a woman's arms,
'Cos de Lord don't like dem feminine charms,
I ain't a'gonna grieve my Lord no more.

But you will get to Heaven in a One-Nine-O,
You ought to see that Jerry go,
O! you will get to Heaven in a One-Nine-O,
You ought to see that Jerry go,
I ain't a'gonna grieve my Lord no more.

Written 1942 *for the aircrew training monthly,* Tee-Emm, *issued by the Air Ministry, and subsequently sung in many station concert party shows. To the tune of " Ten Little Nigger Boys."*

TEN LITTLE PILOT BOYS

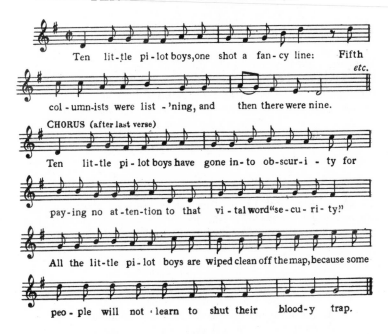

Ten lit-tle pi-lot boys, one shot a fan-cy line: Fifth *etc.*
col-umn-ists were list-'ning, and then there were nine.
CHORUS (after last verse)
Ten lit-tle pi-lot boys have gone in-to ob-scur-i-ty for
pay-ing no at-ten-tion to that vi-tal word "se-cu-ri-ty!"
All the lit-tle pi-lot boys are wiped clean off the map, because some
peo-ple will not learn to shut their blood-y trap.

Ten little Pilot Boys, one shot a fancy line :
Fifth columnists were listening and then there were nine.

Nine little Pilot Boys, one had a heavy date :
The girl was paid by Germany, and then there were eight.

Eight little Pilot Boys, one used a phone to Devon :
The line was an open one, and then there were seven.

Seven little Pilot Boys, one thought his drinks he'd mix :
He talked too much when he was tight, then there were six.

Six little Pilot Boys, in a West End Dive :
One showed-off to a new-found friend, then there were five.

Five little Pilot Boys, discussing fighter lore :
One discussed it much too loud, then there were four.

Four little Pilot Boys, one posted oversea :
Sent a p.c. to his home, then there were three.

Three little Pilot Boys, one talked about a do :
The news was passed across to France, then there were two.

Two little Pilot Boys, eager for some fun :
One spoke about his next-day job, then there was one.

One little Pilot Boy, his mother's favourite son :
She showed his letters to her friends, then there were none.

Ten little Pilot Boys have gone into obscurity,
For paying no attention to that vital word " security."
All the little Pilot Boys are wiped clean off the map,
Because some people will not learn to shut their bloody trap.

––––––––––

The official song of the Air Training Corps, by Charles Dunn, with chorus lyric by F/Lt. Geoffrey R. Edwards, 1166 Squadron A.T.C., 1942. Published by Messrs. Feldman.

WE ARE THE A.T.C.

Very open minded are we in our points of view,
Respected is our name, we always play the game,
Don't think we're superior and you are all taboo,
But let us tell you why we want to make this known to you :
Chorus: We all want to join with the R.A.F.
        Work with the R.A.F., fly with the R.A.F.
        We all want a job with the R.A.F.
        We are the A.T.C.
        We are the A.T.C.
        We are the A.T.C.
        Some of us will go to the Bomber Boys,
        Some to the Fighter Boys,
        Some to the Navy Boys,
        The freedom of the sky to win.
        We are the A.T.C.
        In the Air Force soon we'll be,
        So venture and adventure with the A.T.C.

We are most determined in our zeal to fly a plane,
And high up in the blue, we'll throw a stunt or two.
You will find it difficult our ardour to restrain,
In order to remind you we will mention this again :
Chorus repeat.

A pretty ditty written by Flying Officer F.H. Ziegler and Flight Lieutenant J. A. Atkinson while with 609 Squadron. Sung to the tune of " She had to go and Lose It at the Astor."

HE HAD TO GO AND PRANG 'ER IN THE HANGAR

Prologue: He was a young pilot and when he joined his squadron they gave him their best and newest Spitfire. And before he went up for the first time his Flight Commander said to him, " Jimmie, there you are with your new flying suit, and your new boots, and your new Mae West, and you look lovely. But I do want you to remember everything I've told you, and above all I want you to be very, very careful."

But he had to go and prang 'er in the hangar,
    Forgetting all his teacher's good advice ;
He made a landing slap against the windsock,
    And sat amidst the wreckage in a trice.

The Duty Pilot phoned up his Dispersal,
    His Flight Commander took a gloomy view,
And his C.O., who was watching from his window,
    Said, " Oh, what a very clottish thing to do ! "

Next day he went to see the fierce Group Captain,
    Who said, " It is too big a job for me ;
A flagrant piece of carelessness like this, sir,
    Must come at once before the A.O.C.

" For you had to go and prang 'er in the hangar,
    And though it is the first of your mishaps,
Let me tell you even Wing Commanders Flying
    Are not allowed to land without their flaps ! "

Next day the much be-ribboned Air Vice-Marshal
    Received him with a cold and glassy stare,
And said, " Although to pilots I am partial,
    To let the matter drop I do not dare."

" Why *did* he have to prang 'er in the hangar ? "
    He whispered to the stooge upon his right ;
" The Chief will have to see the boy tomorrow—
    I'll contact him at Claridge's tonight ! "

The C.-in-C. was yawning when he entered,
    And didn't seem to know why he had come,
But when he heard he'd smashed a brand new Spitfire
    He banged his desk so hard he hurt his thumb.

" So you had to go and prang 'er in the hangar—
    You've put up an unprecedented black!
The Air Council are meeting in the morning ;
    If I didn't send you there I'd get the sack ! "

But the Air Council referred the cowering culprit
    To His Majesty himself to judge the case,
For they said that being merely Air Chief Marshals,
    They really couldn't cope with such disgrace.

The " Daily Mirror " featured it in headlines :
    SPITFIRE PILOT SENT BEFORE THE KING ;
The Brains Trust soon decided on the wireless
    If this were treason he would have to swing.

" He had to go and prang 'er in the hangar,"
    The people said from Chelsea to the Strand ;
" Remember, dear, what happened in Malaya—
    Why can't they have a unified command? "

His Majesty was smiling when he entered,
    And offered him a Turkish cigarette,
And said, " I've had to deal with some strange cases,
    But this is quite the most perplexing yet.

" I'm told you had to prang 'er in the hangar ;
    It reminds me of myself when as a boy
They let me go and fly a brand new Sopwith
    Which then was quite the latest kind of toy.

" But I had to go and prang 'er in the hangar,
    And worked myself into a fearful stew ;
But the Wing Commander said ' You needn't worry,
    It's really quite the normal thing to do.'

" And now that you've no stripes left worth the tearing,
    You're free, my fighter pilot, you can go,
But this is my advice : do not go and do it twice—
    Once is quite enough to prang 'er in the hangar ! "

Another version, probably inspired by the first, from 51 Squadron. Composed late 1942 in honour of two crews who, returning from an operation in support of the Commando Raid on the dock gates at St Nazaire, were "foxed" by a rapid change of barometric pressure and crashed their Whitleys into the Yorkshire moors, fortunately without loss of life. Song composed and sung six months after to welcome the crews back to duty.

HE HAD TO GO AND PRANG 'ER
IN THE HANGAR

(Second version)

Prologue : The Wing Commander gathered all his men together and said, " Now chaps, be very careful, especially on return, and for God's sake don't come down through cloud unless you know *exactly* where you are." *But*—there was one stupid clot who had decided to come back early because he had a date with a blonde Waaf. *So—*

He had to go and prang it on the hill-side,
He wouldn't take his Wingco's good advice.
He nearly bought it once before at Dishforth,
And now he's had to go and pay the price.

Returning from a nickel raid on Paris,
The cloud was nearly down upon the deck.
He didn't bother using any Astro,
And now he's gone and broke his blinking neck.

The Wireless Op. was frantic'ly a'tapping,
He wasn't getting any joy at all.
The Skipper said he didn't need a wireless,
And that's a case of pride before a fall.

The Rear Gunner sleeping in his turret
Was not aware that anything was wrong.
He was dreaming of the girl he'd left behind him,
And what he'd have to do to win a gong.

The clock was showing just about nine hundred ;
He thought he'd put it down and have a look.
The Navigator told him not to do it—
It wasn't quite according to the book.

They lost three hundred feet and nothing happened.
He thought he'd put it down a little more.
He knew he didn't really ought to do it—
The Gremlins laughed, they knew what was in store.

The hills just seemed to rise up all around him,
His props were ploughing furrows in the grass.
And when they found them early in the morning
The crew were cut to pieces by the glass.

He had to go and prang it on the hill-side,
He wouldn't take his Wingco's good advice,
He hadn't got the gen, so he went and pranged again,
He had to go and prang it on the hill-side.

----

*When in 1941 in the Western Desert the Air Force heard the German soldiers'
song " Lily Marlene " broadcast from the enemy lines they captured it as
contraband of war ; indeed, it became the Eighth Army's most sung song—
but with different words. Here's one of the more modest airmen's versions.*

TO "LILI MARLENE"

There is a bomber squadron, way up in the blue.
They're off to bomb Benghazi 'cos there's nothing else to do.
They fly all day, they fly all night,
The pale moonlight reveals their plight,
They're going to bomb Benghazi, they're going to bomb B.G.

----

*This is the song of the Guinea Pig Club, which drew its members from officers
and airmen treated at Queen Victoria Hospital, East Grinstead, by the late
Archibald McIndoe, consulting plastic surgeon to the R.A.F. It goes to the
tune of " The Church's One Foundation."*

THE GUINEA PIGS' SONG

We are McIndoe's Army,
We are his Guinea Pigs,
With dermatomes and pedicles,
Glass eyes, false teeth and wigs.
But when we get our discharge
We'll shout with all our might—
" Per Ardua ad Astra,
We'd rather drink than fight."

John Hunter runs the gas works,
Ross Tilley wields the knife,
And if you are not careful
He'll have your ruddy life.
So Guinea Pigs stand ready,
The surgeons call, 'tis said,
And if their hands aren't steady
They'll decapitate your head.

---

*From Central Flying School, Upavon, 1943, by Flight Lieutenant John Mark,
a masterly parody of Noel Coward's " Stately Homes of England." Sung in
a station pantomime by a trio plentifully draped in flying clothing, coloured
scarves and out-size imitation whistles dangling from the top buttons of their
battle-dress . . .*

THE STATELY 'DROMES OF ENGLAND

1st
Verse   Here you see . . . the three of us,
And many a squadron there be of us,
Flyers bold . . . throughout the land,
Our training rigorous and stiff
Should have supplied us with the griff
To do a tour of operations,
Diceing for the Nations.
P.O. Prune . . . the Basher,
Who's sometimes known as the Crasher,
And F.O. Fixe . . . a lad who's grand,
And Sergeant Winde, the bloke who's known as Tail-arse
Charlie,
The Crew is hardly
One you can withstand.

1st
Chorus   The Stately 'Dromes of England, how beautiful they stand,
From Aldergrove to Cranwell and up and down the land.
While at Lulsgate Bottom and Babdown Farm
We discovered the Oxford's wayward charm,
Though it filled us with alarm.
We have mastered it and finally staggered through
A shaky O.T.U.
In Happy Valley nightly,
Or somewhere thereabout,
With Twitch we suffer slightly
But every finger's out.
And wherever we go we always know
We can estimate our track—
Get back to the Stately 'Dromes of England.

2nd   Here you see . . . the pick of us.
Verse You may be heartily sick of us,
      Still with gen we're all imbued,
      We've automatic pilots too
      With which to supplement the crew,
      And many a gadget weird and strange we
      Use upon the Range, we
      Twiddle some knobs . . . and trimmers
      With just some occasional glimmers
      Of language which . . . is rather rude.
      Although we curse and bind about these strange inventions
      Our good intentions . . . mustn't be misconstrued.

2nd   The Stately 'Dromes of England in valley, dale and glen,
Chorus Contain a lot of charming and well-informed young men.
      Though our mental equipment may be slight
      And we barely distinguish left from right,
      We are prepared to fight
      For our principles, though none of us know so far
      What they really are.
      Our duty to the Nation
      It's only fair to state,
      Lies not in Aviation
      But where we aviate.
      And wherever we fly we always cry after many a shaky show,
      Sing Ho for the Stately 'Dromes of England

3rd   The Stately 'Dromes of England are just a trifle bleak,
Chorus From Biggin Hill to Thurso, from Finningley to Speke.
      There's a fellow who wears a gorgeous gong
      For working his Gee-box slightly wrong,
      And he's never been frightfully strong
      On " Performances " . . . a matter for which the clot
      Doesn't care a jot.
      Instead of Navigation we bank on Faith and Hope,
      By casual estimation we always try to cope.
      And wherever we fly we always try
      Whenever we're in the lurch,
      Square search for the Stately 'Dromes of England.

Sung at a Battle of Britain memorial service in Cairo Cathedral, 1943, this hymn was written in a London tube train in July 1940 by Group Captain E. B. C. Betts, and set to music by Flight Sergeant Clifford Barker, then organist at Cairo Cathedral.

HYMN TO AIRMEN

Inspire, O Lord, our men who fly
Their winged chariots on high,
Across the dark and tortured sky.
Take them whereso'er they fare
From all the dangers of the air.

Thy sheltering wings, O Lord, extend,
And succour, help, protect, defend
Where man-made thunders roar and rend.
Give them the only aid that's sure,
A steadfast courage to endure,
The strength of ten that fills the pure.

Bear Thou them up upon their way,
Be Thou their comfort and their stay,
Through perils of their every day.
Grant them Thy shield from all that harms,
And peace at last from war's alarms
Within Thine everlasting arms.

———

This song, possibly of Army origin but a favourite of the Desert Air Force, expresses succinctly the sentiments of many who served in North Africa. To the tune of " Home on the Range."

AFRICA STAR

O give me a bar to my Af - ri - ca

Star, And a clasp to pin on my breast, Then I'll stay here in base with a smile on my face, Con-tent on my lau-rels to rest. Oh,

CHORUS

star, beau-ti-ful Star, I'd ra-ther have beer by far, If you've an

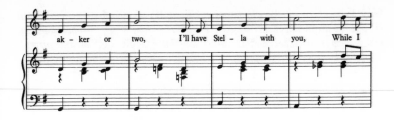

ak - ker or two, I'll have Stel - la with you, While I

tell how I won my Star.

O give me a bar to my Africa Star,
And a clasp to pin on my breast,
Then I'll stay here in base with a smile on my face,
Content on my laurels to rest.

    Chorus : Star, beautiful Star,
                I'd rather have beer by far.
                If you've an akker or two
                I'll have Stella with you,
                While I tell how I won my Star.

Distribution was wide, it spread like a tide,
Like the leaves that come down in the Fall,
For as you can see they gave one to me
And to Naafi and Ensa and all.

    Chorus

Lady Astor herself has one on the shelf
To wear when she puts on her togs,
If you look down the list the only ones that they missed
Were the Jerries, the Eyeties, the dogs.

    Chorus

O give me a bar in my Homeland afar
Where I can show off my Africa Star,
And then I'll confess before they all guess
That I bought it in Shepheard's Bazaar.

Sung by menbers of 285 Squadron while at Woodvale, Andover and North Weald till disbandment at Western Zoyland in June 1945. The squadron, which flew Hurricanes and Oxfords, and later Mustangs, on anti-aircraft co-operation duties, was considered " ropey " because never operational.

WHAT SHALL
WE DO WITH A ROPEY SQUADRON?

We are a ro - pey squad - ron,

We are a ro - pey squad - ron, We are a

ro - pey squad - ron, Ear - lie in the morn - ing.

What shall we do with the Squad - ron Lead - er?

What shall we do with the Squad - ron Lead - er?

What shall we do with the Squad - ron Lead - er?

Ear - lie in the morn - ing.

2nd VERSE

Buy him shares in Hawk - er Air - craft,

Buy him shares in Hawk - er Air - craft, Buy him shares in

Hawk - er Air - craft Ear - lie in the morn - ing.

Chorus : We are a ropey squadron,
We are a ropey squadron,
We are a ropey squadron,
Ear-lie in the morning.

What shall we do with the Squadron Leader ?
What shall we do with the Squadron Leader ?
What shall we do with the Squadron Leader ?
Ear-lie in the morning.
Buy him shares in Hawker Aircraft,
Buy him shares in Hawker Aircraft,
Buy him shares in Hawker Aircraft,
Ear-lie in the morning.

Chorus

What shall we do with our Flight Commander (*twice repeat*)
Ear-lie in the morning.
Give him a flight in a u/s aircraft (*twice repeat*)
Ear-lie in the morning.

Chorus

What shall we do with the binding pilot ? (*twice repeat*)
Ear-lie in the morning.
Send him on a sortie wot he won't come back from (*twice repeat*)
Ear-lie in the morning.

Chorus

What shall we do with the Sergeant Pilots ?
Send them off in very duff weather.

What shall we do with the Engineer Officer ?
Stuff him up with a Merlin XXX

What shall we do with the Officer Pilots ?
Send them off in Mustang Aircraft.

What shall we do with the Canteen Pilots ?
Send them up on Searchlight Co-op.

From 43 Squadron a 1944 version of the old song of the same name. " The beaches " refers to the squadron's numerous invasions, five from Algiers to the South of France.

I WANT TO GO HOME

I want to go home, I want to go home,
I don't want to go up the beaches no more,
Where Focke-Wulf and 88's whistle and roar.
Take me over the sea, where the Messerschmitts can't get me,
Oh my my, I'm too young to die,
I want to go home.

No. 62 was a Dakota Transport Squadron with the Combat Cargo Task Force in Burma. The lyric tells something of the story of the squadron during its Burma tour. 1944–1945. To the tune of " The Road to the Isles."

THE GALLANT SIXTY-TWO

Oh they flapped and they pan - icked in the ar - id Ar - a - kan, They were cut off and they knew not what to do, For the Japs had out - man-oeuvr-ed them (a ve - ry sub - tle plan), So they had to go and call on Six - ty two.

CHORUS
We can fly them in, sup-ply them in, or

drop them from the tow, Though the wea-ther and the Japs may bid us nay, They will be all - right, by day or night, wher- ev - er they may go, For Six-ty - two will al-ways lead the way.

Oh they flapped and they panicked in the arrid Arakan,
They were cut off and they knew not what to do,
For the Japs had out-manoevred them (a very subtle plan),
So they had to go and call on Sixty-two.

Chorus :   We can fly them in, supply them in, or drop them from the
                  tow,
               Though the weather and the Jap may bid us nay,
               They will be all right, by day or night, wherever they may
                  go,
               For Sixty-two will always lead the way.

Then the Japs came a-prancing down the Manipuri Road,
And debouched into the narrow Imphal Plain,
The Brown Jobs were surrounded, when they realised they'd been
   Joed,
Well, they had to call on Sixty-two again.

Repeat Chorus after each verse

The Seventeenth from Tiddim—we sped their hasty way,
The Fifth to plug the Imphal Gap we flew,
And ne'er in Britain's history can anybody say,
So much was done so quickly by so few.

Now Kabaw is a valley, Easy-Easy, a D.Z.,
Where the circuits we admit were rather wide,
Till the Jap one early morning thought he'd show his yellow head,
And shot two down by cutting round inside.

Through rain and cloud or anything you'll always find us game,
Bumps and pockets, hills in mist are our delight,
This last we proved convincingly with devastating aim
On the man who waved the flag upon Fort White.

The Fourteenth reached the Chindwin where they built a Bailey
    Bridge,
Which we shot up very nicely every day,
Like flying fish we followed them, o'er every ruddy ridge,
And set them on the Road to Mandalay.

From Shwebo to Meiktila, Pyinmana to Rangoon
The railways gave our aircrews quite a line,
And we'll fly by day and evening and any bomber's moon,
Till Nippon's Rising Sun sets in decline.

For it's lifts and drops and casualties, and men and mules and post,
Forever till the last trump sounds review,
When Saint Peter fights the Devil and calls up the Holy Ghost,
Why he'll travel in a kite from Sixty-two !

––––––––

This song came into prominence after the Normandy landings in 1945, *when
the 8th Army, like the 14th, rapidly became forgotten. Derivation of the
term " D-Day Dodgers " was attributed (wrongly no doubt) to the late
teetotal Lady Astor. It was adopted as a mark of honour, like " Old
Contemptible," by the British Forces in Italy who considered that the British
Liberation Army and the 2nd Tactical Air Force received undue preferential
treatment compared with themselves. All of this sounds silly in retrospect and
probably was silly then. Nevertheless, " D-Day Dodgers " became an
oft-heard song in Italy. Tune : " Lili Marlene."*

D-DAY DODGERS

We're the D-Day Dodgers out in Italy,
Drinking all the vino, always on the spree.
We didn't land with Eisenhower,
So we fear we're just a shower,
'Cos we're D-Day Dodgers, way out in Italy.

We landed at Salerno, a holiday with pay,
Jerry turned his Air Force out to cheer us on our way,
Showed us the sights and gave us tea,
We all got tight, the beer was free,
We are the D-Day Dodgers, way out in Italy.

Then we got the gen that we were going home,
Back to dear old Blighty instead of into Rome,
But was it that ?   No, oh dear, No,
'Twas Naples first, then Anzio,
We are the D-Day Dodgers, way out in Italy.

You've heard of Lady Astor, our pin-up girl out here,
She is the dear old lady who tries to stop our beer,
And when we get our Astor band
We'll be the proudest in the land,
We are the D-Day Dodgers, way out in Italy.

Then they told us one day we might go into France,
There they said we'd have to fight instead of dine and dance.
But if we went to France we'd have to shine,
You can't do that in a Spitfire Nine,
And we've never seen a Tempest out here in Italy.

Songs of the Parachute Regiment

*The songs that follow in this section were all composed and sung by men of
the Parachute Regiment, jointly trained and organised by the R.A.F. and the
Army.   They came to hand as this edition went to press, allowing no time
to trace authors and provenances.   All are in the airmen's song tradition and
some are variants of R.A.F. songs dating from the " Peace " Years.*

SHEEHAN IS BELIEVING
OR
THIS PARACHUTING BUSINESS

(To the tune of *Mr Gallagher and Mr Sheehan*)

Oh Mr Gallagher, Oh Mr Gallagher,
What is this Airborne Forces thing about ?
Can you give me all the gen
On these parachuting men
And how they're feeling when they're bailing out ?

Oh Mr Sheehan, Oh Mr Sheehan,
The whole darn thing is just a lot of fun,
They go singing at the jump
And they never feel the bump.

I'm astounded, Mr Gallagher.
I'm a liar, Mr Sheehan.

Oh Mr Gallagher, Oh Mr Gallagher,
It is true they practise jumping on the ground ?
Leaping over little things,
Swinging up and down on swings,
And vaulting everything that can be found ?

Oh Mr Sheehan, Oh Mr Sheehan,
To watch their exercises is a joy,
Flying through the air with ease,
Just like mating chimpanzees.

Think of the fun, Mr Gallagher,
Think of the fun, Sheehan old man.

Oh Mr Gallagher, Oh Mr Gallagher,
They jump from a balloon at first I find,
Can they still whip up a thrill,
Or is their first jump just another blind.

Oh Mr Sheehan, Oh Mr Sheehan,
They worry just a little when they're up,
The danger is, you see,
The Y.M. may be out of tea.

Nerves of Iron, Mr. Gallagher,
Throats of leather, Sheehan old chap.

Oh Mr Gallagher, Oh Mr Gallagher,
From rumours that I've heard it would appear,
When a Whitley's overhead,
There's a shout to wake the dead,
Do you think it's the instructor that we hear ?

Oh Mr Sheehan, Oh Mr Sheehan,
It's true they raise their voices now and then,
Just to let the fellows know
If they want to, they can GO ! ! !

On the level Mr Gallagher ?
On the green light Sheehan old man.

Oh Mr Gallagher, Oh Mr Gallagher,
You make the whole thing too good to be true.
Surely something now and then
Shakes these parachuting men,
Is there anything they don't like going through ?

Oh Mr Sheehan, Oh Mr Sheehan,
I'll answer this last question when I'm done,
It's not jumping that's the fuss,
It's the ride home in the bus !

Is it mastered, Mr Gallagher ?
It's a shaker, Sheehan old man.

I'M DREAMING OF A SOFT LANDING

(To the tune of *White Christmas*)

I'm dreaming of a soft landing,
Just like the way we're taught to do.
Feet and knees together, soft as a feather,
It seems so easy after all ;

I'm dreaming of a soft landing,
My thoughts go drifting through the night.
May my first balloon jump be right,
And may all my touch-downs be as light.

YOU'D BE SO NICE TO COME HOME TO

(To the tune of the same)

You're so nice to come down with,
When the aircraft's out of sight,
Up above me you look so lovely,
In your silk gown flowing white,

And it's so nice to see you
And to know you are safe up above,
I'm your paratroop, your my statichute,
Can't live without you my love !

THE MAN ON THE FLYING TRAPEZE

(To the tune of the same)

He jumps through the hole with the greatest of ease,
His feet are together and so are his knees.
If his chute doesn't open he'll fall like a stone,
And we'll cart him away on a spoon !

JUMPING THROUGH THE HOLE

(To the tune of *Knees up Mother Brown*)

When first I came to P.T.S.,
My C.O. he advised
Takes lots and lots of underwear
You'll need it I surmise,
But I replied " By Gad, sir,
Whatever may befall
I'll always keep my trousers clean
When jumping through the hole."

Chorus— Jumping through the hole,
        Jumping through the hole,
        I'll always keep my trousers clean,
        When jumping thru' the hole.

I went into the hangar,
Instructors by my side,
And on Kilkenny's circus
Had many a glorious ride,
On these ingenious gadgets,
Said he you'll learn to fall
And keep your feet together
When you're jumping through the hole.

He swung me in the swings, boys . . .
He shot me down the chute
He showed me the high aperture
I thought it rather cute ;
Said he this apparatus
Will teach you one and all
To centralise your C of G
When jumping through the hole.

I saw the gorgeous statichutes
With camouflage design
I heard the Warrant Officer
Shoot such a lovely line,
" This lovely bit of stuff, lads,"
Said he upon my soul,
" Is sweeter than your sweetheart
When you're jumping through the hole."

One morning very early,
Cold and damp and dark,
They took me in a so called 'bus,
Out to Tatton Park,
In keeping with the weather,
I said to one and all,
" I take a dim and misty view,
Of jumping through the hole."

He fitted me with parachute,
And helmet for my head,
The Sgt. looked with expert eye,
" It fits you fine," he said,
I'll introduce you now to " Bessie "
That is what we call the nice balloon
From which you'll soon
Be jumping through the hole.

"O.K., up six hundred,
Four to drop," said he
" Four to drop, Good God " I cried,
" And one of them is me !"
So clinging very tightly to
The handles on the floor
I cursed the day I volunteered,
For jumping through the hole.

He told me a funny story,
I couldn't see the joke,
In fact I thought he was a most
Unsympathetic bloke,
But when he shouted " Action stations "
Then he shouted " GO !"
I simply couldn't stop myself,
From jumping through the hole.

I hit my pack, I rang the " bell,"
I twisted twenty times
I came down with both feet entangled
In the rigging lines
But floating upside down to earth
I didn't care at all
For I had kept my trousers clean,
When jumping through the hole.

AND HE AIN'T GOING TO JUMP NO MORE

(To the tune of *John Brown's Body*)

" Is everybody happy ? " said the Sgt., looking up,
Our hero feebly answered " Yea " and then they hooked him up,
He jumped into the slipstream, and he twisted twenty times,
    And he ain't going to jump no more.

Chorus: Glory, glory what a hell of a way to die ! (*repeat three times*)
              And he ain't going to jump no more.

He counted loud, he counted long and waited for the shock,
He felt the wind . . . he felt the air . . . he felt the awful drop,
He pulled the lines, the silk came down and wrapped around his legs,
    And he ain't going to jump no more.

The days he lived, and loved and laughed kept running through his
    mind,
He thought about the Medicos and wondered what they'd find,
He thought about the girl back home, the one he left behind,
    And he ain't going so jump no more.

The lines all wrapped around his neck ; the " D " rings broke his
    dome . . .
The lift webs wrapped themselves in knots around each skinny bone.
The canopy became his shroud as he hurtled to the ground,
                  (QUIET)
    And he ain't going to jump no more.

The ambulance was on the spot, the jeeps were running wild,
The medicos they clapped their hands and rolled their sleeves and
    smiled,
For it had been a week or so, since that a chute had failed,
    And he ain't going to jump no more.

He hit the ground, the sound was " splat," the blood went spurting
    high,
His pals were heard to say " Oh what a pretty way to die,"
They rolled him up still in his chute, and poured him from his boots,
    And he ain't going to jump no more.

There was blood upon the lift webs, there was blood upon his chute.
Blood that came a-trickling from the paratrooper's boots,
And there he lay, like jelly in the welter of his gore,
    And he ain't going to jump no more.

R.I.P.

OH MARY THIS TATTON'S A
WONDERFUL SIGHT!

(To the tune of *The Mountains of Mourne*)

Oh Mary, this Tatton's a wonderful sight,
With the paratroops jumping by day and by night,
They land on potatoes and barley and corn,
And there's gangs of them wishing they'd never been born,
At least when I asked them that's what I was told,
The jumping is easy, slow pairs leave them cold ;
They said they'd rather bale out of the moon,
Than jump any more from that awful balloon.

———

BLESS EM' ALL

(Paratrooper's Version)

They say there's Whitley just leaving Ringway,
Bound for old Tatton Park,
Heavily laden with parachute troops,
Bound for the jump that's no " Lark,"
There's many a soldier that's jumped once before,
There's many a one had a fall,
But you'll get no promotion if your chute doesn't open.
So cheer up my lads bless 'em all.

Bless 'em all, bless 'em all,
The parachute packers and all,
Bless all the Sergeants and their paratroops,
Bless all the packers and their statichutes,
'Cos we're saying goodbye to them all,
As out of the Whitleys we fall,
You'll get no promotion if your chute doesn't open.
So cheer up my lads bless 'em all.

———

THE SONG OF THE PARATROOPER

(To the tune of *The Jolly Miller*)

In Henry's day the battle fray,
Was fought with pike and long bow,
And victory was won by he
Who drew the stoutest strong bow,
I'll start my fight with a harness tight,
And a chute packed neat and sure,
And jump to Hell at the Devil's yell,
Through an aircraft aperture.

The nights were bright and tavern's lights
And loud with laughter ringing,
Landlord's wenches, dance and dice,
And rowdy raucous singing,
I'll stake my chance on a Devil's dance
With " D " rings as my daughters
And seek my fun with a Tommy gun,
And heavy duty mortars.

From Plymouth Sound due Westward bound,
Those oaken frigates wallowed,
Up salty green hill, down salt green dale,
While the wheeling sea-gulls followed
I'll sail my sky 'neath a canopy,
Brisk breezes notwithstanding,
And scorn to cuss a sudden gust
And an awkward backward landing.

In days of yore men went to war
On horse back clad in steel,
Or laid along fully fifty strong,
A Norse invaders' keel,
On an airborne ship I'll make my trip,
With the engines steady roar,
Hooked-up strop, then a silk held drop
Five hundred feet or more.

All I ask is the stoutest task,
And a high wide sky above me,
And nine good men for a stick of ten,
And the girl at home to love me ;
And a clean jump through, and a landing true,
And this the vow I've made ;
I'll fight, I'll fly, I'll jump, I'll die,
With a Parachute Brigade.

THE MERRY MONTH OF MAY

(To the tune of *Far, Far Away*)

On her leg she wears a silken garter,
She wears it in the springtime, in the merry month of May,
And if you ask her why the hell she wears it
She wears it for a paratrooper,
Far, far away.

Far away, far away,
      She wears it for her paratrooper
      Far, far away.

Around the park she wheels a perambulator,
She wheels it in the springtime, in the merry month of May,
And if you ask her why the hell she wheels it
She wheels it for a paratrooper,
Far, far away.

Chorus

Behind the door her father keeps a shotgun,
He keeps it in the springtime, in the merry month of May,
And if you ask him why the hell he keeps it
He keeps it for that paratrooper
Far, far away.

Chorus

The paratrooper went to join his unit,
He joined it in the springtime, in the merry month of May,
And if you ask him why the hell he joined it
He joined it to be very, very
Far, far away.

Chorus

In her hand she holds a bunch of daisies
She holds them in the springtime, in the merry month of May,
And if you ask her why the hell she holds them
She holds them for a paratrooper
. . . six feet down.

Chorus: Six feet down,
      Six feet down
      She holds them for a paratrooper
      Six feet down.

YOU DON'T HAVE TO PUSH ME I'LL GO

(To the tune of *You Don't Have to tell me, I Know*)

You don't have to push me I'll go,
The wave of your hand tells me so,
Though I feel in my heart,
That my lines may not part,
If my chute fails to open then
I'll break my heart,
But some day they'll make a mistake,
And the WAAF packer's heart it will break,
For she'll get no promotion if the 'chute doesn't open.
And whether I like it or no,
You don't have to push me I'll go.

———

PASSING THOUGHTS

(To the tune of *John Brown's Body*)

I'd like to find the Sergeant who forgot to hook me up.
 (*Repeat three times*)
For I ain't gonna jump no more.
I'd like to find the WAAF who tied a love knot in my line.
 (*Repeat three times*)
For I ain't gonna jump no more.
I'd like to find the pilot who forgot to throttle back.
 (*Repeat three times*)
For I ain't gonna jump no more.
I'd like to find the WAAF who put the blanket in my chute.
 (*Repeat three times*)
For I ain't gonna jump no more.
Oh they wiped him off the tarmac like a pound of strawberry jam.
 (*Repeat three times*)
For I ain't gonna jump no more.

———

OH COME SIT BY MY SIDE IF YOU LOVE ME

(To the tune of *Red River Valley*)

Oh come sit by my side if you love me,
Do not hasten to bid me adieu,
But remember the poor paratrooper,
And the job he is trying to do.

When the red light goes on we are ready,
For the Sergeant to shout number one.
Though we sit in the plane close together,
We all tumble out one by one.

When we're coming in for a landing,
Just remember the Sergeant's advice,
Keep your feet and your knees close together,
And you'll reach mother earth very nice.

When we land in one certain country,
There's a job we will do very well,
We will fire old Goering and Adolph,
And all of those blighters as well.

So stand by your glass and be ready,
And remember the men of the sky,
Here's a toast to the men dead already,
And a toast for the next man to die.

MEN OF HARDWICK

(To the tune of *Men of Harlech*)

Men of Hardwick never grumble
As their Whitley engines rumble,
Through the hole they gladly tumble,
Ready for the fray.

Laughing as they're downward sweeping,
While the Jerries all are sleeping;
Many Frauleins will be weeping
At the dawn of day.

Battle drums are beating
While the foe is fleeting.
Many Hun will gladly run
And all in disorder retreating.

Downwards, downwards on to glory,
Many the man will tell his story
Of the deeds both dark and gory,
Gallant Hardwick Men.

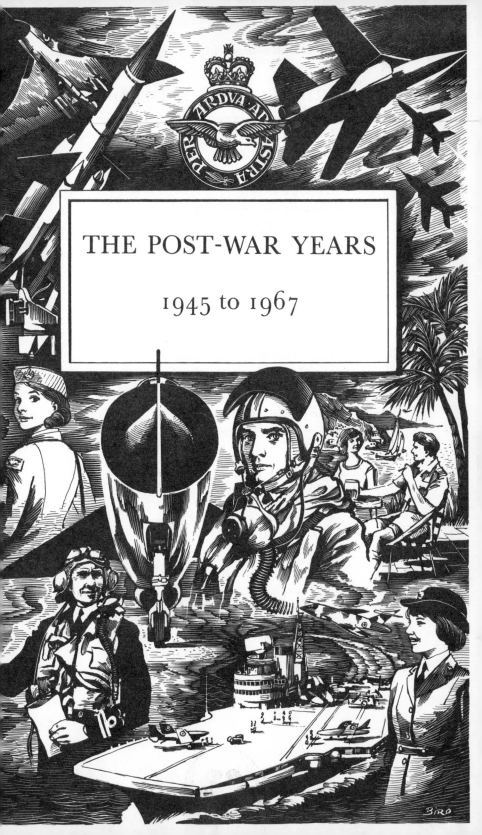

PER ARDVA AD ASTRA

THE POST-WAR YEARS

1945 to 1967

BIRO

THANKS FOR THE MEMORY

Thanks for the memory
Of sunny days in Greece,
The Naafi Desbineese,
The Flirt Bar and the Liberty,
Where drinking doesn't cease,
So thank you so much.
Thanks for the memory
Of double egg and chips,
Routine and some flips,
And all the flap and panic that gave us all the grips,
So thank you so much.

        Athens' Mad Mile and Piraeus,
        Air Marshals who came out to see us,
        Demob forms that promised to free us,
        They weren't quite straight,
        Only three months late,
        So thank you so much.

Thanks for the memory
Of aeroplane repairs,
Without the ruddy spares,
And all the flap and panic,
And Chiefies growing hairs,
So thank you so much.
Thanks for the memory
Of mornings on parade,
The days when we were paid,
And all the guards and duties
We never could evade,
So thank you so much.

        Amendments to Air Publications,
        New leaflets and modifications,
        The number of repatriations,
        But don't be glum,
        Your turn will come,
        So thank you so much.

Oscar Brand, the American folk singer, recorded a selection of U.S. Army Air Force songs (" The Wild Blue Yonder ") for Elektra Corporation culled from a collection made by Captain William J. Starr. The records found their way to R.A.F. Station, Changi, Singapore, where they were played frequently and R.A.F. adaptations were made of two that proved most popular— " Glory, Flying Regulations," which has a fine post-war ring about the lyric, and " Ground Crew," which echoes much the same sentiments on the subject as did songs forty years earlier.

GLORY, FLYING REGULATIONS

The C. A. S. had a fight - ing team that sang a fight - ing song A - bout the wild blue yon - der and the days when men were strong, But now we're reg - u - la - ted 'cos we don't know right from wrong—The force is shot to hell!

The C.A.S. had a fighting team that sang a fighting song
About the wild blue yonder and the days when men were strong.
But now we're regulated 'cos we don't know right from wrong—
The Force is shot to hell !

Chorus :   Glory, Flying Regulations,
Have them read on all the Stations,
Burn the ears of those who break them—
The Force is shot to hell !

Once they flew Mosquitoes through a hell of *flak*,
And bloody dying pilots gave their lives to bring them back.
Now they're playing ping-pong in the Operations Shack—
The Force is shot to hell !
Chorus

I've seen them in their Spitfires when their eyes were dancing flame,
I've seen their screaming power dives that blasted Goering's name.
Now they fly like sissies and they hang their heads in shame—
The Force is shot to hell !
Chorus

One day I buzzed an airfield with another happy chap,
We flew a hot formation with my wing-tip on his lap,
So they passed a new directive and we'll have no more of that—
The Force is shot to hell !
Chorus

So now my eyes are dim with tears for happy days of old,
We loved to take our chances for our hearts were young and bold.
From now on we'll have no choice but to live to be quite old—
The Force is shot to Hell !
Chorus

Sung at R.A.F. Station, Changi, Singapore—an adaptation of a song that originated in the U.S. Army Air Corps.   See note to previous song.

GROUND CREW

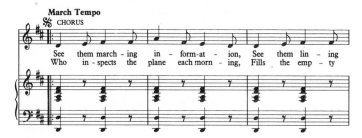

Chorus : See them marching in formation,
See them lining up in grade,
Every day a new vacation,
That's the ground crew on parade.

Who inspects the plane each morning,
Fills the empty tanks at night,
Checks the engines while he's yawning,
Polishes the landing light ?
Watches as the engines rev up,
Hears the motors purr with pride,
Worries as he can't remember—
Did he leave his tools inside ?
Chorus

We have got a little fellow
That the others call the Chief ;
If he lost his Air Force job
He'd have to go out on relief.
Every month he signs the pay-roll,
Every month collects his pay,
Then he goes in hibernation
Till the month has passed away.
Chorus

When we're roaring high in cloud-land,
Hear the engines wheeze and cough,
Watch the wing-tip crack and buckle,
See the loosened prop fall off,
Wonder if the *flak* that sends us
Crashing into land and sea
Gets as many as the Ground Crew—
Aces for the enemy.
Chorus

Still we love the Air Force Ground Crew,
Bless their simple little hearts,
Jumping on our wings and motors,
Eagerly they do their parts.
What if they have their little errors,
They don't do it out of spite,
How we laugh as we're crashing
At the Ground Crew not too bright.
Chrous

———

Penned by L.A.C. Gennis, then of the fire section at R.A.F. Coltishall, with the intention of causing disputation between the R.A.F. firemen and the Gunners who happened to be on the same driving course together at St. Athan. Instead of promoting rivalry, the song had the opposite effect, the Gunners (" Rockapes " apparently from having been stationed at Gibraltar) insisting on its being again and again repeated.

THE ROCKAPE'S DILEMMA

A Fireman and a Rockape met in a mysterious way,
The place was at the Golden Gate,
The time was Judgment Day.
Said St Peter to the Rockape
Who was standing smart and grand,
" What have you done upon the Earth t'gain entrance to this land ?"

" On Earth I was a Gunner,
Travelled many a foreign land,
I tramped along their sandy beach with S.L.R. in hand.
In the name of Queen and Country
I killed at least a dozen men,
In the name of Queen and Country I'd do the same again."

To the Fireman St Peter said :
" I need not ask you aught,
For with your very life you have admission here bought.
On a Royal Air Force Station
A Vulcan crashed that day,
And underneath the Vulcan a Blue Steel bomb did lay.
Although the flames were hot and fierce,
You had your job to do,
You battled through the smoke and flame
To save the five-man crew.
And at this very moment,
At a grave-yard on a hill
The Crash Crew are all gathered to lay your body still.
The bearers of your coffin are the five men you did save,
And not one mortal eye is dry
As your corpse descends into the grave.
So take this harp, brave Fireman,
The Kingdom of Heaven is yours."

And the Rockape watched them enter then
Those slowly closing doors.

———

*This song, attributed to one Corporal Lillywhite, was much sung in Singapore
in the 1950s. It is a pretty accurate account of the units then at R.A.F.
Seletar, and gently highlights the difference between Service and civilian
circles. Verse two alludes to the fact that civilians (and a few airmen) were
sent out by P. & O. instead of by troopship.*

A. C. SOAP

greet his fa - mi - ly. His moth - er - in - law said, "Hey,

while you've been a - way, Tell us what you saw out there."

CHORUS

There's a lit - tle bit of man-grove stretch-ing a - long the shore, A

La - gi bit of man - grove, and then some La - gi more. There's a

fly - ing boat or two, and then there's S. H. Q., A

din - ing hall that's five miles long Where we get the I - rish stew.

Hun - dred Squad - ron, Thir - ty - six, That's the whole damn bag of tricks, Un -

less you add the V. A. F., as well. Then chuck

in H, Q, F, C,, to make the num - ber more,

Put them all to - geth - er, you've got Sing - a - pore.

A.C. Soap, on Southampton Quay,
Put down his kitbag to greet his family.
His mother-in-law said, " Hey,
While you've been away,
Tell us what you saw out there."

Chorus :   There's a little bit of mangrove stretching along the shore,
A *lagi*[1] bit of mangrove, and then some *lagi* more,
There's a flying boat or two, and then there's S.H.Q.,
A dining hall that's five miles long where we get the Irish
    stew,
100 Squadron, Thirty-six, that's the whole damn bag of
    tricks,
Unless you add the V.A.F.[2] as well.
Then chuck in H.Q.F.E., to make the number more,
Put them all together, you've got Singapore.

Little Jimmy Jones went to Singapore
On an ocean liner, nothing could be finer.
When he got back home
His folks began to ask,
" Tell us what you saw out there."

Chorus :   There's a Concrete Lizzie[3], looking very busy,
Roaming round the air base with concrete in her hair.
There's a Tuan Besar[4] in a highly polished car
Driving round his offices to find out what his profit is.
Take some Tamils and some Greeks, add some Siamese and
    Sikhs,
And of course innumerable Chinese,
Then add in a few Malays to make the number more,
Put them all together, you've got Singapore.

1 **Lagi (Malay)** – more
2 **Straits Settlements Volunteer Air Force**
3 **Concrete Lizzie** – Chinese woman labourer on building site
4 **Tuan Besar (Malay)** – Big Boss

––––––––––

*Quick march ditty sung when the 2nd Tactical Air Force was equipped with
Sabre aircraft from the U.S.A. in the 1950's.*

SABRE SONG

Break Left,
Break Right,
Streamers on the wing.
Flick roll,
Slow roll,
We do anything.

We're the Joy Boys, the Joy Boys,
The Boys of Shiny Two.
We never, never worry
'Cos we all know what to do.

This duet, to a sprightly, original tune, deserves to go down as an R.A.F. classic along with such evergreens as " Bless 'Em All," " The Bold Aviator," " The Ballad of Sulaiman " and " Those Shaibah Blues." Characteristically, it comes from a station very much " out in the blue "—R.A.F., Gan, a staging post in the Maldive Islands, Indian Ocean, 2,500 miles equi-distant from Aden and Singapore. Tours of duty there are limited to one year, are unaccompanied, and the island is woman-less. Originally sung in a pantomime there in 1960, lyric by Flight Lieutenant H. A. Philbrick (Signals) and music by Squadron Leader Victor B. Kendrick (Education). It proved so popular that it was orchestrated by Flight Lieutenant N. J. Warnes, M.B.E., L.A.R.M., A.R.C.M., as a march and added to the repertoire of the Far Eastern Air Force Band, Singapore. The last three dedicated verses were for Officers' Mess use only.

SONG OF THE TWO SAD FLIGHT SERGEANTS

(" The Gan Song ")

Tempo di Marcia

Here we are, spend-ing a year on Gan,

Pass-ing three hun-dred and six - ty five days get-ting a won-der-ful tan.

Here we are spend-ing a year in the sun,

258

*u/s = unserviceable

1. (*Together*)
Here we are, spending a year on Gan,
Passing three hundred and sixty-five days getting a wonderful
   tan.
Here we are, spending a year in the sun,
Catching a glimpse of a woman when we can.
We've got to be contented if we want to keep our minds,
We've got to buy from NAAFI 'cos there are no other kinds,
We've got to do our flipping job or else the C.O. binds—
There's another u/s Britannia on the pan.

2. (*1st Sad Flight Sergeant*)
Look at me, waiting to leave at last,
Hoping I get a Comet 'cos the Brits aren't very fast.
Look at me, longing to join my wife,
Waiting to have the holiday of my life.
I've got to wait for my relief, but still he hasn't come,
I've got to keep on working 'cos he will not leave his mum,
He thinks he's bloody clever, but I think he's just a bum,
But I'm thankful that my celibate year has passed.

3. (*2nd Sad Flight Sergeant*)
I'm new to this, I've only been here a week,
And from my first impressions it's a place that's pretty bleak.
I'm new to this, sweating beneath the sun,
In short I'd say I'm really up the creek.
I stopped a night in Aden and I've got Khormaksar gut,
I bathed without my flip-flops and I've got a coral cut,
I met a girl in Blighty who was very lovely but
I've got to pay her seven-and-six a week.

4. (*Together*)
Here we are, spending a year on Gan,
Passing three hundred and sixty five days getting a wonderful
   tan.
Here we are, spending a year in the sun,
Catching a glimpse of a woman when we can.
We're very short of money 'cos we get no L.O.A.*
We spend our evenings in the bar a-squandering our pay,
We wake up in the morning when we hear the Tannoy say :
" Get up to work as quickly as you can. . . .
" There's another u/s Britannia on the pan . . ."
So we'd better fix the bastard if we can.

5. 205 *Squadron* (*regular visitors from Singapore*)
    Here we are, the Shackleton stand-by crew,
    We're hanging around the bar because we haven't a thing to do.
    Here we are, whooping it up on squash,
    For alcoholic liquor is taboo.
    We're here for Search-and-Rescue but we rarely get a call,
    In fact the Brits and Comets never trouble us at all,
    The only thing that makes us feel like climbing up the wall
    Is when our Flight Commander's passing through
        (We're never certain what he's going to do,
        He's sure to finish up in Timbuctoo).

6. *Gwen* (*first women welfare worker on the island*)
    Here I am, they wrote me a verse in the song,
    I'm on a tropic island though I never wear a sarong.
    Here I am, trying to help the boys
    By putting things to rights when they go wrong.
    They thought by coming here I might improve the way they
        live,
    But I can't help them very much, I've no alternative,
    The only thing they really want I'm not prepared to give,
    Or I wouldn't be staying here for very long.

7. *Vic* (*the Composer, on posting*)
    Here he goes, for nearly a year he's been
    Singing to us on Saturday nights " The Ballad of Bethnal
        Green."
    Here he goes, heading for Uxbridge Town,
    Meeting up again with Padre Dean.
    He's been our Educator and he's done a wizard job,
    Teaching the Maldivians at thirty bob a nob,
    We're very sad to lose him and we can't repress a sob,
    For we're going to notice his absence from the scene.

Local overseas allowance

BRIEF GLOSSARY OF TERMS

A.C.	Aircraftman
A.C.2	Aircraftman Second-class
A.C.3	Aircraftman Third-class (mythical)
A.C.H./G.D.	Aircrafthand/General Duties
ACK-EMMA	Air Mechanic (1914-18)
A.C.W.2.	Aircraftwoman Second-class
ADASTRA HOUSE	Air Ministry
AEROS	Aeroplanes
A.G.s	Air-gunners
A.H.Q.	Air Headquarters
AIR BOARD OFFICE	Great War equivalent of Air Ministry
AIR OBS	Air-observers
AKKER	Coin
ALBACORE	Fleet Air Arm aircraft
ALBATROS SCOUT	German fighter
A.M.	Air Mechanic (1914-18) ; Air Ministry
A.M.O.s	AIR MINISTRY ORDERS—"A" series (permanent), " N " series (temporary)
AMMO	Ammunition
ANEROID	Aerial barometer
ANSON	Reconnaissance aircraft
ANTI-DIM	Substance for preventing dimming of anti-gas respirator eye-pieces
A.O.C.	Air Officer Commanding
ARCHIE	Anti-aircraft gun or fire (1914-18)
ARGENT	Money
A.T.C.	Air Training Corps
A.T.S.	Auxiliary Territorial Service
AVRO	Trainer aircraft
B.1, 2, 3, etc.	Balloon sites
BAG	Score
BAKSHEESH	Alms
BALLOONATIC	Any officer, airman or airwoman in Balloon Command
BANDIT	Enemy aircraft
BANK, TO	To dip a wing
BASKET	A euphemism
B.E., B.E.2, B.E.2c	Bleriot Experimental scouts (Great War)
B.G.	Benghazi
BIGHT	Loop of a rope
BINGE	Party
BLENHEIM	Medium bomber
BOMBAY	Troop-carrying aircraft
BOSTON	Bomber
BRASS HAT	High-ranking officer
BRISTOL FIGHTER	Fighter aircraft of late Great War and 1920's
BROWNED OFF	Fed up
BROWN TYPE	Soldier
BUMP	Air pocket
BURST	Of gunfire
BUS	Aeroplane
CAMEL	Sopwith's premier Great War fighter
CARDINAL PUFF	A pernicious drinking game
CARRY THE CAN, TO	To take the responsibility
C.B.	Confined to Barracks (obsolete in R.A.F.)
C.C.	Confined to Camp
CHIEFY	Flight Sergeant
CHITTIES	Notes or written papers
CHOTA DROP	Little drop
CLEARANCE	Clearance from debts, i.e. of mess bills, library books, etc.
CLOT	A mass of material stuck together (*Oxford Dictionary*)
C.O.	Commanding Officer
COMMANDO PIANO	Instrument specially built to withstand punishment
CONKING	Breaking down
CRACKERS	Mad, crazy
CRACK-UP	Accident (especially to aircraft)
CRAMMER'S PUP	Pupil being prepared for an examination
CRASH GUARD	Guard placed over a crashed aircraft or vehicle
CRATE	Obsolete aircraft
D.C.s	Transport aircraft
DECK	Ground
DEFFY TWO	Defiant II aircraft

DEMAND	Requisition form
D.H., D.H.4, D.H.9, D.H.9a	Bomber aircraft (Great War and after)
D.I.	Daily inspection
DIAL	Face
DISPERSAL	Area in which aircraft are parked wide apart
DITCHED	Forced descent into water
DOPE	Half-wit
D.R.O.s	Daily routine orders
DROME	Aerodrome, airfield
DUFF	Dud, no good
DUTY FLIGHT	The flight of airmen (whether of the flying or earth-bound sort) who are on duty
E.A.	Enemy aircraft
EGGS	Bombs
ENSA	Entertainment National Services Association, a department of N.A.A.F.I. (which see)
ERK	Aircraftman or aircraftwoman, i.e. of rank below corporal
EYETIES	Italians
F.E., F.E.2b, FEE	Farman Experimental reconnaissance aircraft (1914-18)
FELUCE	Money
FITTER D.P.	Fitter and driver of petrol-propelled vehicles
FITTER ONE	Fitter Group 1
FITTERS A.E.	Aero-engine fitter
FLAK	Anti-aircraft fire, especially from enemy guns
FLAMING FOUR	D.H.4
FLAP	Excitement
FLIGHT MECH	Flight mechanic
FLIMSIES	Thin papers for carbon-copying notes, capable of being chewed and swallowed in emergency
FLIPPERS	Ailerons
FLOP	Failure
FOKKER, FOKKER MONO	German scout (Great War)
FORTRESS	Heavy bomber
FUKA	A landing ground in North Africa
GAS	Gasoline, petrol
G.D.	General Duties (i.e. flying and other duties) ; ground defence
GEN	Genuine information
GNÔME	A type of aero-engine commonly used in the Great War
GONE FOR A BURTON	Dead, killed
GOOFA	Boat, ship, troopship
GRAVY	Petrol
GREENHORN	Novice
GREMLIN	Mythical sprite on whom airmen blame their troubles
GROG	A drink of spirituous liquor and water
HAD IT	Not had it, failed to get it, lost it, missed it
HALBERSTADT, HALBERSTADTER	German reconnaissance aircraft (Great War)
HAM-HANDLE	Handle ham-fistedly
HANDLEY	Handley Page bomber
HARD TACK	Stale bread, ration biscuit
HARRY TATE	R.E.8 reconnaissance aircraft and trainer
H.D.	Home defence
HERCULES MARK THREE	An aero-engine
HOT AIR	Wasted breath, line shooting
HOTCHKISS	Machine gun ; engine
HUDSON	Coastal Command reconnaissance bomber
HUN	German ; flying pupil ; trainer aircraft
HURRICANE	Fighter, fighter-bomber
INSTITUTE	Airmen's canteen
IN THE BAG	Accomplished, achieved
I.O.	Intelligence Officer
JANKERS	Fatigues
JERRY	German
JINK, TO	To evade enemy fire by swinging from side to side
JOY-STICK	Aircraft control column
JUNKERS 88	German bomber-reconnaissance aircraft
KITE	Aeroplane
KITTY, KITTIES	Kittyhawk aircraft

Konk Out, To	To fail (especially of engine)
K.R.s	King's Regulations & Air Council Instructions
L.A.C.	Leading Aircraftman
Le Rhone	Type of aero-engine used in the Great War
Legs Eleven	11 Squadron (from an expression in the Service game Housey-Housey)
Lewis	Machine gun
Line	Boast
Line Shooter	Boaster
Maknoon	Mad
Martinet	Trainer aircraft
Master Three	Trainer aircraft
Maternity Jacket	Royal Flying Corps tunic
M.E.	German Messerschmitt fighter
Met	Meteorological service
Mhutti	Dirt
M.O.	Medical Officer
Monosoupape	Type of aero-engine used in the Great War
Moskeen	Broke, without money
M.T.	Mechanical transport
M.U.	Maintenance Unit
N.A.A.F.I.	Navy, Army and Air Force Institutes
N.B.G.	No bloody good
N.C.O.	Non-commissioned officer
N.F.T.	Night flying test
Nieuport	French single-seater scout (Great War)
Nine A	D.H.9a (which see)
Number Two	Co-pilot or second pilot ; second in command
O.P.	Observation patrol (Great War)
Ops Room	Operations Room
Orderly Bloke	Orderly Officer
" P "	Personnel
P.B.O.	Poor bloody observer
Pecker	Nose
Peechi	Soon
Per Ardua Ad Astra	Through Labour to the Stars
Perim	Perimeter (of airfield)
Pfaltz	German scout (Great War)
Plonk	Aircraftman Second-class
Plotter	One who plots the positions of aircraft on a large-scale map
Pongo	Soldier
Popsy	Girl friend
P.O.R.s	Personnel Occurrence Reports
Post, To	To transfer from the pay strength of one squadron or unit to that of another
Prang	Break, destroy, damage
Prop	Propeller
P.R.U.	Photographic Reconnaissance Unit
P.T.	Physical training
Puma B.H.P.	An aero-engine
Pup	Pupil ; or Sopwith Pup aircraft (Great War)
Put up a Black, To	To make a mistake
Q.D.M.	A homing bearing
Q.F.E.	Barometric pressure at aerodrome level
Quod	Detention, guardroom, prison
R.A.F.	Royal Air Force ; Royal Aircraft Factory (Great War)
Raf	Aeroplane engine designed by the Royal Aircraft Factory (Great War)
Records	Records Office (which controls postings, promotions, etc., of all airmen and airwomen)
R.E.8	Reconnaissance trainer (Great War)
Revs	Revolutions
Revving	Accelerating
R.F.C.	Royal Flying Corps
R.I.C.	Royal Irish Constabulary
Richthofen	German air ace of the Great War
Rigger	Airframe fitter, Group II, or flight mechanic
Ripline	A cord for removing the rip panel from a balloon, thereby deflating it.
Rookie	Recruit

Ropey	Unsatisfactory
Rumpety	Maurice Farman " Shorthorn " aircraft (Great War)
S.17	Site 17
Scouts	Reconnaissance-fighter aircraft (Great War)
Screw Picket	A type of peg for mooring purposes
Scrub	Wash out, abolish, delete
S.E.	Fighter (Great War)
Second	Second ring, i.e. flight lieutenancy
Service Institute	(See " Institute ")
Servicing	Flight of ground personnel who service aircraft
Sheds	Hangars
Shoot a Line, To	To boast
S.H.Q.	Station headquarters
Site	An area of ground (a station is made up of sites 1, 2, 3, 4, etc.)
" Ski "	Whisky
Snipe	Sopwith single-seater scout
Snoop, To	To pry into
Sop, Sopwith Camel, Sopwith Scout, Sopwith Pup	Fighters (Great War)
S.P.	Service or Station Policeman
Spad	French fighter (Great War)
Spit	Spitfire fighter
Split-Arse Cap	Field service cap
Split-Arse, To	To stunt aerially
Sprog	Airman under training
Stalag	Military prisoner-of-war camp (German)
Stick	Aircraft control column
Stooge, To	To do unimportant work
Straffed	Attacked
Stung	Pained
Stunt	Any out of the ordinary event
Switch	Bomb release
Syndicate	Conveniently-sized body of pupils
T.A.B.T.	Vaccinations and inoculations
Tac/R	Tactical reconnaissance
Tail-end Charlie	Air-gunner in rear turret of bomber
Tit	Button, i.e. firing button of machine gun
Tomahawk	Fighter aircraft
Tour of Ops	Tour—or regulation period—of operational duty
T.R.9	Ground-to-air intercommunication by radio
Twin H.P.s	Twin-engined Handley Page aircraft
Two-Five-Two	Form 252—Charge Sheet
Typhoon	Fighter aircraft
Undercart	Undercarriage of Aircraft
Vickers	Gun ; aircraft
W.A.A.F.	Women's Auxiliary Air Force or members thereof
Wad	Cake ; bun
Wadi	Dried-up water-course
Whitley	Heavy bomber
Wid	Member of Women's Division (Canadian)
Wimpey	Wellington bomber aircraft
Wing Commo	Wing Commander
Wing H.Q.	Wing Headquarters
Wizard	Wonderful
W.O.1.	Warrant Officer First-class
Wom	Wireless-Operator-Mechanic
Wop	Wireless Operator
W/Op., Wireless Op	Wireless Operator
W.T.	Wireless telephony
Y.M. Hut	Canteen run by Young Men's Christian Association
64	Form number of an Airman's Service and Pay Book
252	Form 252—Charge Sheet
2C	B.E.2c aircraft
2E	B.E.2e aircraft
9A	D.H.9a aircraft (Great War)
100 Octane	Aviation petrol
664B	Form 664B—Voucher for charging for loss of or damage to equipment
765C	Form 765C—Flying Accident or Forced Landing Report